DAD CALLS ME JACK

Happy reading!

Eugene L. Vickery, M.D.

(Jack)

DAD CALLS ME JACK

by
Eugene Livingstone Vickery

******

Foreword by George Eells

******

Illustrations by Douglas Vickery

******

Cover Design by Judy Kohn and Douglas Vickery

STONEHAVEN PUBLISHERS
602 Oak Street
Lena, Illinois 61048
******

Published by:
Stonehaven Publishers
602 Oak Street, P.O. Box 367
Lena, Illinois 61048
(815) 369-2823

Cover design by Judy Kohn and Doug Vickery

Printed in the United States of America.

Library of Congress Cataloging in Publication Data

Vickery, Eugene Livingstone. 1913-
    Dad Calls Me Jack.

    1. Vickery, Eugene Livingstone, 1913-   —Childhood
and youth.   2. Lena (Ill.)—Biography   I. Title
F549.L53V53   1986   977.3'33042'0924 [B]   86-14326
ISBN 0-937775-00-2

Dedicated

to

Mother and Dad

With Love and Appreciation

CONTENTS

ILLUSTRATIONS

Twelve Photographs follow last chapter

ACKNOWLEDGEMENTS

An opportunity to acknowledge the abundant help I have received is one of the real pleasures of writing this book. Millie, my wife, is one whose inspiration and stimulation led to the book. She also did the typing, editing and public relations. I am deeply grateful.

Our four children, their spouses and eight grandchildren have a certain responsibility. The stories were written for them and their enthusiastic responses kept me at it. It must be obvious that I owe much to my parents and to the friends of my boyhood who figure so prominently in my memories.

Lois Kortemeier is a beloved friend and diminutive dynamo who had the cheery confidence and encouragement to help us see the project through. Julie Martoccio, lawyer, columnist and longtime friend offered insistent urging that I write and keep writing.

Lucy Miele, well-known midwestern writer, entertaining lecturer and dear friend, not only appreciated the stories and encouraged me, but helped predict problems and smooth the road. Ruby and Bob

Ziegler have given both unwavering support and the most delicious pheasant dinners.

Adrianne and Alan St. George are close friends whose artistic evaluation and enthusiastic responses were important.

George Eells, magazine editor and author, nationally-known for his numerous fascinating biographies of entertainment stars, has my deep and lasting gratitude for his many years of friendship, sympathetic encouragement, and for his foreword to this book. As another Northwestern Illinois boy, he understands the era and the area involved. I have learned a great deal from George, not only about writing and publishing, but also about the power of pleasant persistence. By the way, he was a scout in Canyon Camp when I was Chief Pioneer.

Special appreciation goes to our daughter Michelle, a CPA, who arranged for publication of this book and took care of many details. I am particularly glad that our son Douglas, MFA, a professional artist, provided the artistic illustrations. Our daughter Anita, physical therapist, and our physician son, Jack, have helped with understanding and eagerness for additional stories.

Lowell Moss Publishing Services have earned this public recognition for their skillful behind-the-scenes professional efforts to bring you DAD CALLS ME JACK.

FOREWORD

These reminiscences in DAD CALLS ME JACK
vividly evoke what it was like growing up in a small
town in the midwest before the advent of electronic
entertainment made imaginative play less important.
In those days, children had to invent their own ways
to amuse themselves. Luckily, Dr. Eugene Vickery's
total recall provides a treasure-trove of incidents,
games, fads, styles, people and even brand-name
products that make these sketches as much fun to
read as a visit to the Smithsonian.

Eugene Vickery grew up in Lena, Illinois, ten
miles from Winslow where I was born, so we enjoy
many shared memories. Since he was eight years
older—a lot when you're children—I didn't know him
personally then, but he was such a high-achiever that
like many people all over Northwestern Illinois I had
read about him in the Freeport *Journal-Standard*.
Throughout Stephenson and Jo Daviess counties, he
represented the shining example of youth that parents
hoped their offspring would turn out to be. His
adventurousness, high scholastic attainments and pre-
eminence in the Boy Scouts (he eventually became

a Silver Palm Eagle Scout) made him a role model—
not that we had ever heard of the word back then—
for boys throughout the area. He was obviously a
young man who could go wherever he chose.

The few years difference in our ages put us in
different worlds then. Even though I generally spent
a couple weeks each summer in Lena with my Uncle
Cash, Aunt Rosetta and cousins Marjorie and
Virginia, Vic and I never ventured more of an exchange
than "hello" as we passed on the street.

Then in the early 1950's when I was living in
New York and Los Angeles, I began hearing from
my mother and my sister what a brilliant doctor Vic
had become and how lucky it was for people from
Lena, Winslow, Stockton, McConnell, Warren and
other towns that he had decided to carry on the
tradition established by his great grandfather and
father rather than accept an appointment to the staff
of a famous medical center in the East. Gradually
I learned that during World War II he had been
Executive Officer to the Chief Surgeon and had written
a two-volume history of the United States Army
Medical Corps in the Middle East.

It was not until 1971, after my New York doctor
retired and I was due for my annual physical, that
I visited Dr. Vickery professionally. I remember not
only being impressed by his thoroughness, but also
by his willingness to examine exaggerated as well as
justified health concerns. Lena, I decided, was lucky
not only to have a skilled medical man, but a gifted
psychologist as well. So valuable did I regard his
expertise that a 4,500-mile, round-trip visit to the
doctor did not seem unreasonable to me.

Both his patients and his colleagues obviously shared a high opinion of him. In 1981, he was selected by the Academy of Family Physicians as "Family Doctor of the Year" in Illinois and he was featured as one of the ten finalists in the national "Family Doctor of the Year" competition in an article published by *Good Houskeeping.*

Gradually, the medical help he was giving to my family and me ripened into a personal friendship with him and his wife, Millie, a dark-haired charmer who is as intelligent and vivacious as she is beautiful. If I never entirely overcame my dread of professional encounters with Vic—or any doctor—I certainly looked forward to spending time with the Vickery's at their Apple Canyon Lake home whenever I visited Illinois.

Vic and Millie's four children were out on their own by the time we became friends. I was fortunate enough to get to know young Jack, but under the most tragic circumstances. My sister with whom I was very close was terminally ill in Rockford Memorial Hospital where young Jack was serving a gruelling medical externship in another department. Yet no matter how late the hour nor how long his day had been, Jack never failed to put in a daily appearance in my sister's room to pass a cheery word with her and any of the rest of the family who might be present. Obviously, he had absorbed his parent's caring attitude. Fittingly enough, on the day that Vic turned over his practice to a new doctor in Lena, young Dr. Jack began work as a neurologist at a Harrisburg, Pennsylvania neurology group.

Once retired, Vic decided to expand his literary output beyond the rhymed report on the family that for so many years he and Millie had sent to friends each Christmas. When he began setting down these memories of a happy childhood, they were intended only for his grandchildren. But as he finished one, the idea for another would pop into his mind and he would write it down—sometimes in prose, sometimes in verse. After the number of pieces exceeded twenty, Vic and Millie's artist-son, Douglas, volunteered to illustrate them. Now with DAD CALLS ME JACK, all of us can relive, or share for the first time, how it felt to grow up in a small Illinois town before radio and television homogenized America.

Surrender then to the experience and enjoy Vic's book.

George Eells

George Eells is an author and biographer of the stars. Editor of Theatre Arts Magazine, then of Signature, he also worked for Parade Magazine. Eells was entertainment editor for LOOK Magazine and wrote for "This is Your Life" television show. His books include THE LIFE THAT LATE HE LED, a biography of Cole Porter; HEDDA AND LUELLA, produced as a movie for television in 1985 starring Elizabeth Taylor and Jane Alexander; GINGER, LORETTA AND IRENE WHO?; MERMAN (with Ethel Merman); HIGH TIMES, HARD TIMES (with jazz singer Anita O'Day); and MAE WEST (with Stanley Musgrove). Eells' latest book is a biography of ROBERT MITCHUM.

PREFACE

Last year I retired from my practice of medicine as a family physician and started my second childhood. I think I am better prepared for it than I was the first time. However, I am not familiar with all these electric, electronic and complex mechanical, transformable toys. I do remember very well the simpler objects we used for play and learning and the fun we had. These stories come from a brief period in the boyhood of a child who grew up in a respectable wood frame house occupied by a family headed by a country doctor in an American midwestern village.

The East has given us much of our origin and history, the West adventure and exploration. The South gave us elegance and romance. Mid-America has supplied stability and abundance. No features are exclusive and together they create a unique balance.

I feel only mildly apologetic about the relatively inconsequential fact that this boy, writing his contemporary stories, is sixty years late.

Eugene L. Vickery, M.D.

INTRODUCTION

There must have been a big commotion in our house the morning I was born. Mother has told me about it. She worked awfully hard to have me and in the morning Dr. Brown came to help her. It was in a little white house in Fairmount, Indiana, on Thanksgiving Day.

She said my head was bruised and swollen and I was red and wrinkly, but she loved me. She held me a little while and then gave me to my dad, saying, "Otis, here is your son. Now you can give him his name."

Dad said, "Thank you darling, with all my heart. You know the names I have been thinking about. I want us to call him Eugene, which means 'the well-born.' Then I would like for his middle name to be Livingstone, in honor of Dr. David Livingstone, the Scottish medical missionary and explorer in Africa." Mother agreed and that is the way I was named.

Ever since then, Dad has called me Jack.

Eugene Livingstone Vickery

FISHING WITH
MY DAD

Dad and I are going fishing this afternoon. He said he'd take me and I know he will, if he doesn't have to look after someone who is hurt or sick.

It's July and hot and getting dry. We would have gone this morning when it was cooler, but somebody called and Dad had to take care of a lady who was sick. That's the way it is when you are a doctor and somebody needs you. He knows how to help people and I am glad he does. But I sure hope we will get to go fishing this afternoon. Anyway, I've got my good old dog, Pal, to wait with me. He is a beagle and he likes to chase rabbits, but in the hot weather he likes to just lie down and pant, too.

Maybe after a while we will go into the little woods at the back of our lot. We will see how the chickens and ducks are getting along. My dad has a flock of chickens which he likes. They are big chickens called Buff Orpingtons and they remind him of when he was on the farm, he says. There are some ducks in the flock. They are called Mallard ducks and a farmer gave them to Dad. They are supposed to be wild and would fly away except the farmer

3

clipped some feathers off one wing of each duck. They like it here where they can be sure of getting something to eat, but sometimes I think they would like to fly away. Right now they have some little ducks. They are called ducklings and they are fuzzy and cute but awfully wiggly when I try to pick them up.

It won't be long till we go fishing. My dad is a good fisherman. Once when I was little he took me fishing in a creek on Grandfather Vickery's farm. Dad called it "the Home Place." That is where he was a little boy and it is in Indiana. We live in Illinois now. There was a wooden bridge across the stream. Right near it were some trees and Dad cut two branches with his pocket knife. He cut off the leaves and tied a string to one end of each branch. Then he put a cork bobber on the strings and tied a fishhook on the end of each one. He kicked over some dirt along the creek and got some worms to put on the hooks and then we fished in the creek. We caught some fish, but they weren't very big. I think they were sunfish or something like that. We fished there for a while and he would help me pull in a fish and take it off the hook. It was fun, but I got tired and I think maybe he liked fishing more than I did.

Now I'm nine years old. I have strong muscles. Dad tests them once in a while, and he says I have. I won't get tired now. I really want to go fishing with Dad. He said we would go to the Kettle Hole in Yellow Creek. I hope it will be afternoon real soon.

****

Oh boy, did we have fun! Dad took me fishing just like he said. We rode out to the Kettle Hole in his Ford Model T roadster. It is the one he makes calls in when the roads are good enough. Otherwise he rides a horse or a bobsled. I am almost big enough to drive it, but I don't think I can crank it yet. He said the Kettle Hole is near Kent and it is a place where Yellow Creek makes a bend and gets real wide. There are lots of trees with good shade and the grass is long and soft. There was some wind so it was not too hot along the bank of the creek. It was just wonderful! We walked along the creek for a while, looking at the pretty water and the birds and some cows not far away. We took Pal along. He likes to ride in the car and run in the fields and wade in the water. He didn't hardly chase the cows at all.

Dad got out his fishing tackle box and the two long bamboo poles he bought at Pappy Wingart's store. He showed me how he tied his fish line to the pole and put the wooden bobber on so we could tell if a fish was biting, and then he tied a fishhook on the end of the line and squeezed a lead weight on above that to hold it down where the fish could get at it. I fixed mine just like his. Then we dug some fish worms with a little shovel he brought and we baited the hooks. That's what he called it. But I was not good about squishing the worms onto the hooks and Dad said, "Better let me do it, Jack. You might get a fishhook in your finger." It was all right with me for him to put the worms on, but I don't think I would have hooked my finger. My name isn't Jack, of course, but that is what he always calls me. If anybody else said that, I wouldn't know who he meant.

5

Mother calls me Bill, but that isn't my name either. All my friends call me Vic; that is the same nickname my dad had.

Well, we were out there a long time and maybe we did not catch many fish, but we got a few. Some we threw back because they were too little, but we brought home three and the biggest was one I caught. It was over a foot long and it was a bullhead. I pulled it in all by myself, but Dad helped get it off the hook and into a bucket of water to bring home. We moved to different places around the Kettle Hole and sat on the grassy bank. Our fishing poles reached clear out to the middle of the water. After we tried all the places it was late so we came on home.

Boy, were we thirsty! It was hot and we did not want to drink the creek water because of the cows using it. We had a canteen of water to start with, but it did not last very long. All the way home I was thinking how much fun it was to go fishing with my dad and how glad I would be to get back to that good old pump in our back yard. As soon as we got home we jumped out and ran across the yard to the pump. I had a head start because I was on the right-hand side of the car and there isn't any door on the left side. It is just stamped to look like a door. Anyway, Dad got to the pump almost as soon as I did and he started pumping. Pretty soon the cold water came out of the spout and we splashed it all over our faces and arms and then we ran it into the big old tin cup and took turns drinking out of it.

Pal was so glad to be home he ran and tried to drink water with us. He likes to go with me and when I am gone without him he misses me. Even when

I am at school, but now it has been a long time since school.

Dad and I skinned the three fish we brought back and that is really a chore. We had to pull the skins off with pliers. Then Dad cleaned out their insides. Now I know how, I guess, but I don't like that very much.

Mother was happy to see us and said she would cook the fish in corn meal batter. She did, and oh, boy, that smelled good! They tasted just as good, too, but we had to be awfully careful of bones.

Now it is almost cool and quiet, except for mosquitos humming and Pal panting. The sun went down just back of our backyard and it was beautiful, shining through the trees and on our garden. I was so happy I wanted to tell Dad, but he had gone to help someone who was sick.

DAD BROKE
THE COWCATCHER

My dad is what they call a country doctor. He takes care of sick people. We live in town, but sometimes he goes to the country to see people who are sick or hurt and can't get to town. Sometimes it happens at night.

He cranks up his Model T Ford roadster and puts his medical bag in the trunk in back and drives out to the patient's house. A good friend of his, Dr. Alzeno, a dentist, often goes with him at night. He either helps or just goes for the fun of it. Anyway, Dad says it is safer that way, because the car can break down or they can have other kinds of trouble and it is better if there are two of them.

Last night Dad had a "hurry-up" call to see a patient near Eleroy. Dr. Alzeno went with him and they were going lickety-split down the road when they got to a railroad crossing. They had to go up a steep grade to get to the railroad tracks and then the road turned to the right to go along beside the railroad. There was a light down the tracks, but they thought they had lots of time.

The car went up the steep little hill and its motor died right on the tracks. Then they could see that the light was the headlight on a big freight train coming right at them. There was no time to crank the car motor to get it started. The train was coming from the right, so Dr. Alzeno opened the door on his side and jumped out toward the train and rolled down the hill. My dad was on the driver's side of the car and it doesn't have any door. So Dad had to jump out the right side door after Dr. Alzeno and just as he got out and started to roll down the hill the train hit the car.

There was a big crash and the trainmen stopped as soon as they could but it took a long time. Then they came back to the wreck. They thought the people would be dead in the car, but Dad and Dr. Alzeno were scrambling up the hill. The trainmen were glad to see them. The engineer did not see them get out and he thought for sure they were in the car.

The car was a wreck, but Dad got out his doctor's bag and it was all right. Not even a bottle of medicine was broken. Then they looked at the engine of the train and the step which was part of the cowcatcher on the front was broken off.

The trainmen asked them to ride back to Lena in the caboose, so they did. Then Dad called Mr. Ellis from Kennedy and Ellis Ford Garage to come and tow in the wrecked car. Mr. Ellis came in the old Stevens wrecker they have and took Dad back to make his call. Dr. Alzeno went home to bed. He thought that was more sensible.

After Dad made his call, he and Mr. Ellis hooked the Ford onto the wrecker and towed it back to the garage. Dad came home and Mother wondered why it took him so long to make a call.

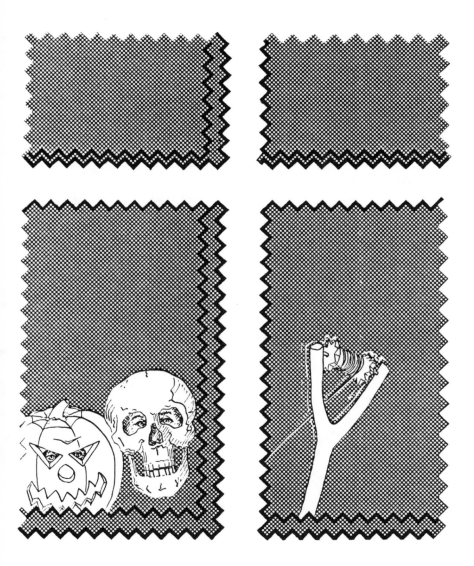

HALLOWEEN

It is not really late yet, so I think I will write something about Halloween. It is this evening. In school our teacher told us the "een" is a conrtraction of "evening" and should be "e'en." It used to be a "holy evening" and that is where the "hallow" part comes from. Tomorrow, November 1, is "All Saints' Day." I guess it is a general purpose holiday. If the church forgot any Saint during the year, he would not be mad.

For some reason kids everywhere do lots of tricks on Halloween. They try not to get caught, but even if they do, nobody punishes them unless it is something awful or hurts somebody. The weather is cool and windy. It is wet under foot but not raining now.

Baldy, Woody and I went out about six-thirty. It was dark. Lots of porches and windows had jack-o-lanterns. They were bright but sort of spooky with flickering candle light. At our house Mother and Dad helped us make three. Dad had brought home the pumpkins. Mother cut lids out of their tops and lifted them up by the stems, and then cut off the inside stringy stuff and made notches so if we wanted to put the lid back on when a candle was burning, it could get air. Then she let Virginia and Margery and me scoop out the seeds and the stringy yellow stuff from inside the pumpkin. When it was all hollowed out, she drew funny eyes, nose, mouth and even ears on it with a pencil. Then she used a paring knife to cut through the pumpkin's wall on the pencil marks. When we lit the candle she put inside, the face showed up even in the dark. She let me make the next one and then the third one. Virginia helped and Margery watched. They thought it was fun and didn't care if it was scary.

When it was dark, Mother took two of her house plants off their stands, set jack-o-lanterns on them and put them where they could be seen in the windows. She and I set the biggest one on the front porch.

Baldy and Woody and I wanted to play a few tricks before the party. We had our pockets full of tiny little rocks to throw against window panes to scare people. Each of us had some kind of window rattler. I made mine by cutting off a small tree branch that had a fork, just like for a sling shot. I got a big spool from Mother and whittled notches on the edges and strung it between the branches of the fork on a wire. Then I tied a long string to the spool and wrapped it around and around the body of the spool so that when I pulled on the end of the string, it would make the spool go around fast. All I had to do was hold the handle, press the spool against a window and pull the string. It really rattled the window. Each of the others had something like that. Some kids just took sticks to hit the windows. Of course, we all had bars of soap in our pockets.

The party was at the Lutheran Church. We had plenty of time, so we went to about ten houses on the way and rattled windows and yelled, "Whooo, whoooeee" or made noises like owls, dogs or wolves. We could usually see in the windows enough to know if they were startled or scared or did not pay any attention. The ones that did not seem to notice anything were usually the ones who found soap marks on their windows later.

Just before we went in the church for the party we put masks over our faces. Mine was like a skull, Woody's looked like a jack-o-lantern and Baldy's was supposed to be a ghost. We got them at Pappy Wingart's. Some of the little kids were in costumes and masks. Most of the high school boys and girls wore eye masks of different colors on their faces. Some were in costumes and some not. There were a few grown-ups who were putting on the party. They did not wear masks. Everybody was moving around, talking and laughing and guessing who their friends were.

Three big tubs of water had apples floating in them. Different sizes of boys and girls were at different tubs, bending over to try to bite an apple and get it out of the water without using hands. Then they set up two teams, one boys and one girls, to do a relay race. The first one on each team had to get an apple out of a tub with his teeth, then let the next one on the team take the apple by biting it. The second person then ran to the chair and back and let the third one take the apple by biting it. That person ran to the chair and back, and so on. There were five on each team and no one dared to use his hands.

It was a lot of fun, but so mixed-up we could hardly tell what we were doing. The grown-ups tried to keep it straight. There were several sets of teams, each set with one team of girls and one boys, and all about the same size. In a regular race we could have beat the girls, but in the apple race they beat us. They were serious about passing the apple from one to another, but we got to laughing.

They had other games. One was like pin the tail on the donkey, but using a big black cat. There were circles where they played "spin the bottle," and one time they made a big circle of Sunday school chairs for "musical chairs." Someone played the piano and someone pulled one chair out of the circle during each strain of music. When she stopped playing, somebody in the marching circle would not have a chair to sit on and he was out. It was taking too long so they started removing two or three chairs at a time.

The party was over about eight, but they had cookies and punch afterward. We stayed for some of that, then went out to walk around town to see what was going on. We ran and then stopped in the shadows to watch the big guys. There were two or three gangs of high school boys around town doing tricks. Quite a few people have bathrooms in their houses, but there are also many outside toilets or outhouses. We watched one group of three or four boys push on several outhouses in different parts of town. A couple they tipped over and others they moved off their bases. If some people have to go out later tonight they will be surprised. Woody and Baldy have theirs indoors. They thought it was funny. I just hoped nobody would tip ours over.

There were a few pumpkins smashed on the streets and there was a lot of window-soaping and weird noise-making.

The best stunt we saw was when we were about ready to go home. We went past the schoolhouse. The two outhouses back of the school, one for boys and one for girls, were too big to tip over or move, but they were all covered with toilet paper, crepe paper and newspapers. On the front steps of the school, right by the door, we saw a bunch of big guys pull up a buggy and turn it on its side to block the door. We watched till they left. By that time we were tired and cold, so we split up and went home.

Now I am warm and comfortable. Mother fixed some warm cider. She and Dad and I sat in the front room for a while. They told me about Halloween pranks they did when they were young. It made me feel good to hear them. I do not think it was much different then.

CACTUS CAME
HOME ALONE

We just had an ice storm and everything is so slippery you can hardly walk anywhere. It is supposed to be spring but the ice storm came and made it look like winter again. All the tree limbs and twigs have ice on them. The sun is out and the trees look like glistening lace. Mother said they sparkle like diamonds and I think I know what she means, but I never saw a diamond. I think it looks like stars in the daytime, if you were up close.

This morning early Dad had a call to see someone who is sick out in the country. So Ma fixed us all some bacon and eggs and milk and homemade bread and jam for breakfast. Then Dad put on his short overcoat and his fur cap. He went to our little barn where Cactus was in the box stall and told him they were going for a ride. Cactus is a big tan-colored horse who grew up out west. Dad said he was trained for riding by a cowboy who called him Cactus because he was hard to ride. He doesn't much like to have his bridle put on. He tosses his head, but he does stand still so Dad can get the bit in his mouth and the bridle around his head. The horse's head is a lot higher when he swings it up, so Dad has to slip the bit between his teeth and put the straps over his ears real quick when his head is down between tosses. After that it is easy.

Dad has a McClellan saddle. He said it is the same kind they used way back in the Civil War and was first made for General McClellan. It is lightweight, covered with rawhide leather and has an opening in the middle for the horse's backbone. Dad put a saddle blanket on Cactus, then swung the saddle over and tightened the cinch belt under his chest. Cactus tried to hold his breath with his chest big, so the belt wouldn't be so tight when he let up. Dad said, "That is a trick he learned, but if I let him get away with it, the saddle will roll over because the cinch isn't tight enough." So Dad poked his knee against Cactus' chest and he let out a big whoof. Then Dad tightened the cinch real quick.

Dad got his saddle bags and fastened them on behind the saddle. They hold all the medical things he needs when he goes to see patients. When the roads are good, he uses his Ford roadster, and then he takes his regular black bag. When the roads are bad because of snow, he has someone drive a cutter, which is a sleigh, or sometimes a bobsled for him. Then he also takes his black bag. He only uses the brown leather saddle bag when the roads are sort of in between and he rides a horse.

This morning he and Cactus went slowly because of the ice. There are ice shoes for horses, Dad said, but Cactus just has regular shoes on, so it is slippery for him, too. Cactus was sort of jumpy. Dad said, "He is feeling his oats because he hasn't been exercised the last couple of days. Too stormy." They went up the hill to Lena street then west out of town.

It wasn't very long till I heard a noise outside. I ran to the window and looked out. It was Cactus all by himself stomping on the ice and bumping the barn door. He looked all right and the saddle and saddle bags looked like they did before, but Dad was not anywhere around.

Mother was worried. "What could have happened?" she asked. Then we put on our overcoats, hats and galoshes and went out to get Cactus into the barn. He wanted back in his nice warm box stall with straw on the floor. It wasn't hard to make him walk through the doors and back to his own place. Mother just took the saddle bags off and left the bridle and saddle on. "I just wonder what happened to Otis," she said. That is my dad's name.

By the time we got to the house, Dad was coming back, cutting across Downing's yard. He was limping and was not very happy. He came in the house and took off his boots and coat and his fur cap with the flaps and his gloves. We hugged him and asked if he was all right. He said he was, but his whole left leg hurt. He said, "We were doing all right until the edge of town. Then a rabbit ran across the road and that blamed horse spooked. He reared right up and then slipped and fell down. He fell on my left leg, but luckily I was partly in the ditch. It could have been worse. He scrambled up and got away before I could catch him. I wasn't moving very fast."

Mother said, "I'm glad you were not hurt any worse. Have some coffee and warm up, then you can decide what to do next. Cactus is in the barn."

Dad said, "Well, if he is all right we will just try it again, I guess."

And that is what they did. Then, after the call, Dad went to his office. But this evening he can hardly move his leg, or stand on it either.

FLOODED BASEMENT

Our town is on high ground and we do not have a river to flood us. But there are several hills in town and sometimes water runs down the hills and into the basements of houses in the valleys. It has been raining a lot this spring, really a lot. Our cellar has about two feet of water in it. It is up to the fire box of the furnace. It is lucky that the weather is warm enough so we do not have to have the fire in the furnace.

Mother hates it and Dad doesn't like it very much either. But my sisters think it is fun and I do, too. I found some small boards and sawed off pieces of wood to look like boats, then I whittled on them to shape them up better until we had a regular fleet of little battleships and gun boats. I used nails for guns. Then I took Virginia and Margery down the cellar steps very carefully. They had to sit on the steps, but I rolled up my knickers, took off my shoes and stockings and waded in. They put the boats in the water and pushed to make them go. When they stopped, I pushed them back or gave them to the girls to start over. We sailed them for a long time and made some new ones to add to the fleet. Mother looked down the stairs once in a while to see if we were all right.

Dad came home. He looked down to see what we were doing. When he saw the biggest boat I had made, which was about three inches wide and ten inches long, he said, "Say, if you'll give me that one I think I can make an engine for it."

"Swell," I said and waded out to get our biggest battleship.

He took two tongue depressors out of his bag and tacked them along each side of the back of the ship's deck, so they stuck straight out behind with a couple of inches of space between them. Then he took another tongue depressor out of his bag and whittled it into a paddle like a paddle wheel. He found a couple of rubber bands in his bag, too. He put them on the first two pieces to go across the space between them. Then he put the paddle between the strands of rubber band where it could be wound up. When I saw what he was doing, I said, "Oh, let me do it. I see how it works."

He handed it to me and I wound it up and set it in the water. I was so anxious to do it I forgot to figure which way to wind it. The boat went backwards. But it went nice and fast. When it was unwound the paddle floated free, I picked it up and wound it again, but this time made it go forward. The girls were real tickled with it and I liked it, too. I thanked Dad and he said, "You're welcome. Just be careful down there." Then he went on.

FLOODED BASEMENT

We found out that it can be fun to have a flooded basement, but it does not take much playing down there to be enough. It takes a long time for the water to drain out and for the basement to dry. It is a mess.

CORNET LESSON

I am just back from taking my cornet lesson and my lips feel thick. They are not really sore, but they are still weak because I played the cornet so much. My teacher says if I would practice more my lips would not get so tired. I guess he is right. He knows a lot about it. His name is Maurice Sprague and he paints houses inside and out and helps take care of the school house sometimes. He knows about music, even violins. He is the director of the town band.

He lives over by the Methodist Church. When I go for my lesson it is usually after school or sometimes on Saturday. I put my beautiful silver cornet in its case, fold up my music stand and put that in its case, take my music and put them all in my coaster wagon. Then I either pull or pedal it up the hill past the railroad passenger depot and on for another block to the church corner, then go to the left to his house. Mrs. Sprague is nice and sometimes she gives me a cookie, but not till after I am through with my lesson. I have been playing the cornet about a year now. I think I have played an awful lot of scales and hit the notes pretty well, even if I have not practiced as much as I was supposed to. He is starting to give me more regular pieces to play and maybe next year I can play with the school orchestra. I am working on the "The Carnival of Venice" and some Sousa marches.

My cornet is called a B-flat and A, like most of them. It can be changed from one to the other by a switch that lets the air go, or not go, through a loop of pipe. I have to play the notes just as they are written because I can't transpose. Aaron plays the violin and he knows how to transpose, so he can play along no matter how the piece is written.

Woody plays the clarinet and he is getting good at it. He sucks on the reed and gets it all wet, then puts it in the mouthpiece before he starts to play. It sounds hollow and soft, and there is more fingering to do on a clarinet. I like having just three valves to press down to make all the different tones. Then, too, I can leave all the valves open and play it like a bugle. Sometimes I like to play it way down low, with my lips loose. Then it sounds like a big raspberry, but I guess that is not very musical.

Mr. Sprague taught me how to blow air in the mouthpiece to make the tones. He told me to put my upper lip over one-third of the opening and my lower lip over two-thirds of it, then blow into the horn moving my tongue as if I were spitting a little thread off the tip of my tongue. It worked and now I can get clear sharp tones that I like to hear. I hate to make a mistake because it sounds bad and you can hear it a long way away. If they make a mistake on the clarinet or violin it is not so noticeable.

Baldy doesn't play any instrument, but he sings really well in class. He remembers songs the best of any of us. My Dad got a two-tube Crosley radio and sometimes we listen to it, taking turns with the ear phones. We like to hear orchestras play and different men and women sing. When they sing new songs, Baldy always seems to know them first.

Another thing we like to do is keep track of the stations. Sometimes we write a postcard to KDKA or WLW or some of the others and tell them we heard a program at a certain time. They send us a postcard saying that was right and this confirms that we really heard them. Some guys collect confirmation cards from all over. I don't have very many.

Sometimes when I am practicing I get to fooling around with the mute to make different sounds. Trumpeters in orchestras use them for special effects, but Mr. Sprague has not really taught me how to use it yet. My mother plays the piano and sings and my dad sings in a baritone voice. In school we have music classes and learn about tenor, baritone, bass, soprano and alto. My little sister Virginia is not really big enough to sit at the piano, but she likes to try to play and Mother is teaching her something about it. I think the cornet is better for me. One note at a time is plenty.

When I was coming down the hill toward home, I saw Miss Helen King in her yard. She waved and I waved and stopped. She asked me what I was doing. I told her I had just had a cornet lesson. She teaches fifth and sixth grades and knows Mr. Sprague. She said, "Oh, that's good. What did you play today?" I said, "We worked on scales and tonguing and slurs and little quick grace notes and lots of stuff like that." Then I got out my cornet and showed her how they went. She thought that was nice and I got in a little extra practice.

At the bottom of the hill I left my wagon at the front of the steps, took all my things in and yelled, "Hey, Ma, I'm home." Ma said, "Come on back to the kitchen. I'll bet you would like some cookies and milk." I didn't tell her Mrs. Sprague had given me some already. Anyway, I was hungry for more.

SKATING BOARD

This morning Baldy called and told me his dad had just given him a new pair of roller skates. His old ones were worn out in the clamps and straps, but the wheels were still good. He said, "Why don't you come over and we'll try to make something out of the old skates?"

I said, "Sure," and pretty soon I was riding my bike up the hill, across the tracks and out to his house almost at the end of Oak Street. It is a small gray house.

His mother, Mrs. Estelle Baldwin, is a nice cheerful lady, but she does not let Baldy keep anything around the house that he is not using. Sometimes he would like to have souvenirs or make collections, but she does not want to have things clutter up her house. His father, Mr. Leslie Baldwin, is strict, too. He works at the Lena State Bank. Most people call it the Baldwin Bank because Mr. George Baldwin, Baldy's grandfather, has a lot of stock in it and is an officer of the bank. My dad bought a little bank stock, but not very much.

DAD CALLS ME JACK

We went to the shed in back of the house. Baldy showed me the new skates and the old ones, which his mother said he should throw away. He said, "The wheels are all right. If we nail the foot plates of a skate to the front and back of a board we can have fun with it, and Ma won't make me throw it away, since we'll be using it."

"Great," I said.

Everything in the shed was neat. We found a hammer, saw, nails, and some good boards right away. "Would your dad let you use these?" I asked.

"We will be very careful," Baldy said.

We took one skate apart, cut off the worn strap, and nailed the back of the skate to one end of a board about three inches wide and two feet long. Then we nailed the front end of the skate to the front end of our board. "Now," Baldy said, "we need a board to come up in front."

He took another three-inch board and sawed it off about three feet long and nailed it so that it came up at the front of the foot board. I found a two-inch board we could saw and use to brace the upright board and also to nail crosswise at the top to make a handle bar. We put everything away and swept out the sawdust, then he took the skating board out to the sidewalk.

He put his left foot on the footboard, held the handle bar and pushed with his right foot. It went just fine. He worked up speed with it then coasted. It was not very good on corners, but he could lean it around some or just step off and swing it. He let me try it and I thought it was fun. "I've got another skate and more boards," he said. "Let's make you one." We did and that used up the morning.

I left my bike at his house and rode the skating board home. It was so rattly on the sidewalk I could feel it all over. Something a little strange happened on the way home. I crossed the railroad tracks as usual between the freight depot and the passenger station. There was no train, but several boxcars were standing on the siding by the freight depot. Lots of times we kids walk along beside the big cars to see what they have or if any one is unloading them.

The cars must have been left there during the night. No one was working on them and the second one seemed to be empty. I heard a noise in it, like a cat meowing. The door was just open a crack and I thought I could see something, maybe a cat. I could not move the door.

Mr. Charlie Salisbury was on duty in the station. He is a telegrapher. He uses the telegraph key to send telegrams and to tell where the trains are or when they are going to arrive. He was on duty the night my dad first came to Lena and let him sleep on the big table in the station till morning.

He is friendly, but he always stays close to the telegraph instrument in case there would be an emergency. He said, "Hello, Eugene, what can I do for you?"

I said, "I'm all right, but I think there is a cat in that second boxcar."

He said, "Well, let's go see."

He pushed the door open enough to look and at first nothing happened. Then, all of a sudden, a big cat jumped out of the boxcar to my shoulder, then to the ground and ran away. Even though I thought it would be a cat, it startled me and Mr. Salisbury, too. He looked all around in the car and then said, "That's it, I guess. I wonder where he came from?" He went to the station.

I rode the skating board all the way down hill. After lunch I walked back for my bike and took my time riding it home. The skating board is fun, but I think I like skates better.

SCHOOL DAY

Today it was mostly sunny and the ground has dried since the spring rains. It was a school day but nothing special happened. I think I will see what it is like to write about a day with nothing special.

This spring I am finishing the fourth grade. Last fall I started in third, but third and fourth are in the same room and Miss Mary Perkins teaches both of them. I learned the third grade stuff all right, but I found it was more interesting to listen to the fourth grade and watch what they were doing on the blackboard. After a while Miss Perkins talked to my mother and said that since I was a little old for the third and young for fourth, why not see if I could do both grades this year. Dad and Mother said, "Why not?" and asked me about it. I was not sure what all I would have to learn to catch up with the regular fourth graders, but thought it would be all right.

Miss Perkins said I should practice the multiplication tables at home with Mother and the rest she would teach me in school. So that is the way it worked. Miss Perkins is a wonderful teacher, sort of strict but kind, and you can tell she really wants you to learn. She is not married and does not have any children of her own, but I think she likes all of us a lot. My first and second grade teaacher was Miss Edna Dunn and she was wonderful, too. I had her for two years and the only thing I don't like about skipping a grade is that I will only have Miss Perkins for one year.

Classes went along as usual today. A nice thing about school is recess. We have recess morning and afternoon and that gives us a chance to play outdoors unless the weather is too bad. When it is warm, like today, we do not have to wait to put on coats or rubbers, we just run outside and get started at whatever we want to do.

One of the games we like to play is Pom Pom Pullaway. Near the front door, on the way out, someone yells, "Pom Pom Pullaway!" Then everyone who wants to play runs toward the east side of the playground, away from the highway, and half of them line up on the sidewalk facing the school. The rest line up along the playground near the school facing the other line. One or two go out in the middle and yell, "Pom Pom Pullaway, if you don't come I'll pull you away!" One or more at a time then try to run from their line to the other one without getting tagged. If a runner is tagged or touched by one who is "It," the runner stays in the field and tries to tag other runners. Sometimes the best runners like to be "It" to start with to show off how good they are. Finally everyone is in the middle of the field and no one is left to tag so the game is over. The last one tagged is the winner, but it is often hard to tell.

Another game we like is Andy Over. We go to one of the outhouses and line up about ten boys and girls on each side of the building, a few steps away from it and facing it. Each outhouse is the same on the outside, but one is for boys, the other for girls. For some reason we usually play Andy Over at the boy's house. They are longer in the north-south direction and have regular roofs with ridges in the middle slanting down toward each side. Ordinary outhouses have slanted, flat roofs with the higher edge in front so it does not dump the water down your neck when it is raining. I do not know what the girls' house is like on the inside, but the boys' has places to sit down along one side and along the other is a trough which slants down so several sizes of boys can use it at the same time. The wall behind it is covered with tin so a fellow does not have to hit the trough exactly.

To play Andy Over, somebody has a rubber ball. When the sides are lined up on each side of the house, the one with the ball yells "Andy Over" as he tosses the ball over the roof. If someone catches it, everybody on that side tries to run past the middle line between sides before being tagged by someone from the tossing side. Those tagged go out of the game. The next toss over the roof is done by someone of the first catching side. They do this until everyone on one side is out of the game.

We have other kinds of tag. Sometimes we form a large circle of boys and girls, all facing the center. The first one who is "It" starts running around the outside of the circle. He touches someone on the back and that person has to run around the circle the opposite way. The one who gets back to the empty place first can stay in it and the other one is "It." There is usually too much standing around with this one.

Grab-and-Run is another sort of game. The first boy or girl grabs something, a pencil or pocket knife or anything, from a second one and yells and runs with it. The second one chases till he gets it back. Usually boys do that.

We always have rubber balls, baseballs or softballs with us. It is easy to play catch with one or more of the guys. If there are several interested, we usually get a bat from Mr. Hoppe or a teacher and start a baseball game. If there are enough we have teams, if not we play work-up with three, four or more. All of them are fun.

Mr. Hoppe is the school janitor. He is so strict that we think he is mean. I suppose it is hard work trying to keep the building clean with so many kids running around.

We had music today, in our room. Miss Florence Lampert comes and takes charge of all the children in the room for singing and learning about staffs, notes, time, chords and voice parts. I like music class but some of the fellows don't. Miss Lampert is pretty and nice. Her father is the mayor and postmaster.

This afternoon in recess we played some games, but most of the kids had their roller skates. The school yard takes up almost a whole block. There is a lot of sidewalk to skate on. We skate fast and slow, play tag and swing-along. It is fun.

Just before school was out the superintendent came to our room for a visit. His name is Mr. Frank

Donner and he is in charge of the whole school, high school and all. Once in a while he visits our room to see how things are going. He is pleasant, but you can tell he is the head of it. Everyone is very respectful. He did not stay very long. After talking with Miss Perkins, he looked at us and smiled and told us to study hard.

After school I skated through town on the way home. I had a nickel so I stopped at the Opera House Cafe and bought an Eskimo Pie. I ate it on the way home and it tasted good. That is how it was on a day that was just about like all the rest.

WAGON WHEEL

This was a great day. It is Saturday. We were out of school on a sunny spring day and it felt good. Baldy came over early and while we were in the yard talking about what to do, Woody came. He was all dressed up as if he were going to Sunday school. That made us wonder, because we were in overalls.

He had to see Dr. Tucker, the dentist, at 11:30 a.m., and his mother thought he should look nice for that. It was only ten o'clock and he had his bike. So we rode our bikes up the hill together to the railroad station. Dr. Tucker's office is above the Lena State Bank just south of the station, but it was too early to go there. Woody said, "Let's go watch Mr. Schulz."

That was something we liked to do and he never seemed to mind. He is called a wheelwright and he works in a small building behind his house. His shop is back of Taylor's Store, on the highway. He keeps hard white oak boards and big pieces of wood in the shop. He says that he picks out the pieces very carefully to be sure they do not have knots or weak spots, then he seasons them by letting them dry for several years before he uses them. I don't know how he can tell so far ahead how much he will need. I suppose he makes about the same number of wheels every year. He makes strong wooden wheels with steel tires for farm wagons and buggies.

There are more and more automobiles and trucks every year, but every farm has horses and wagons. Some families use buggies, sleighs and bobsleds for short trips, even if they have a car. When the weather is bad the car cannot get through the country roads anyway. So Mr. Schulz keeps busy making new wheels. They "take a lot of punishment," as Dad says, but sometimes they wear out or break.

At his long workbench, Mr. Schulz has vices and special tools he uses to shape the oak wood into a big hub, spokes and a round heavy rim. He cuts wood into rough shapes with a saw then shaves them with drawing knives until they look right to him. He measures to be sure, but most of it he can tell just by looking at a piece because he has done it so many times. He puts the pieces together and hammers them in place and there it is, a nice big new wagon wheel.

He lays the wheel on the ground out by the highway and builds a round, low bonfire on the ground not far from the wheel. He has plenty of wood chips and pieces for the fire, which is like a circle on the ground without any fire in the middle. It is about the size of the wheel and when it is burning evenly all around he lays a steel hoop in it. The hoop is made of strap steel, just the size of the outside edge of the wooden wheel. Mr. Doll, the blacksmith who has a shop across the street, helps by making the steel tires.

As soon as the steel tire is warmed by the fire to make it expand, Mr. Schulz picks it up with tongs and quickly puts it on the wheel. It goes over the wood and he looks at it very carefully and makes sure it fits just right everywhere. As the steel cools it tightens on the wood. When it is really cooled down a person could not ever get it off without heating it again. That is why the steel tires stay on and the wheels last so long.

This morning he was just finishing a wheel and that was a good time to watch. He said, "Hello," but we could see he was paying very close attention to his work, so we stayed out of the way. After he put the steel tire in place and it started to grab the wood, he smiled and said, "There, that makes another one. Well, how are you, boys? What are you up to today?" We said we were just riding our bikes and we liked to stop and watch him work.

"You're welcome to watch," he said. "But as soon as this one cools a little more I'll hang it on a peg and go in for a cup of coffee. I might start another one this afternoon if I feel like it then." When he went in the house, we looked at the tools and wood and wheels, then went across the street to watch Mr. Doll in his blacksmith shop.

That was different. The wheel shop was clean and smelled like wood. There was a little wood fire smoke out in front. The blacksmith shop was open, but it seemed dark inside because it was sooty. The forge was going strong and Mr. Doll used the bellows to make it real hot. There was a big horse in the shop. The farmer who owned him was standing by his head so the horse would not get excited. The horse did not seem to be jumpy at all. He probably remembered having new shoes before. He was one of a team; the other horse and the wagon were outside the shop along the highway.

Mr. Doll pounded on the red-hot iron horseshoe till he shaped it the way he wanted, then he dropped it in a barrel of water beside him. Heating and sudden cooling tempered the steel and made it tougher. He heated and cooled it several times, then took the shoe and a hammer, put some horseshoe nails in his mouth between his lips and bent over by the horse's left front leg. This is called the "near" front leg; the other is the "off" one. He was facing the rear of the horse. He bent over, brought the horse's foot up between his own legs, held it there with his knees, put the shoe in place and nailed it on right through the outer edge of the hoof. Then he took a clipper out of the pocket of his heavy apron, clipped off the ends of the nails even with the hoof, and set the horse's foot down. It did not take long. The horse stamped his foot a time or two as if he were testing it and then stood quietly.

The blacksmith shop smells of fire, scorched horse hooves, harness and horse manure. It is not bad, but I don't think any other place smells quite like it.

We did not stay very long because Woody thought it would be fun to see if Mr. Diestelmeier was working in his harness shop. Some of the kids call him Old Henry, but he is a nice man who makes harnesses and bridles and things for horses in his shop, just a block east of Taylor's Store on Main Street, beside the railroad. His shop is full of leather gear hanging up and on stands and racks. It is a little dim, but we could see all right as soon as our eyes got used to it. It smells good, like tanned leather. A saddle was on a sawhorse just inside the shop. He does not make saddles but repairs them.

I guess he knew we were not customers. He just said, "Hello, boys" and kept on working. He was cutting a heavy strap to fit on a harness that needed a new buckle. We could tell he liked to work with leather. When he took the new strap over to the harness he said, "That is good belt stock. Oak-tanned, full-thickness cowhide." He used a punch to make holes in the new belt to fit those already in the harness, and then cut a place for the tongue of the buckle. He used an awl and heavy waxed linen thread to fasten the new piece to the old. Then he tested the old strap in the new buckle and said, "It fits fine, but I think the other strap will wear out pretty soon. I'll replace that, too."

We did not watch that, because Woody had to hurry to get to Dr. Tucker's office. He is pretty strict and Woody might have trouble explaining how he could leave home at ten and be late for an eleven-thirty appointment. Baldy and I rode to the dentist's office with him, but we did not want to wait inside. "Let's go see the horses," I said. Baldy said, "OK," so we went across the street and just south from the bank, behind Stadel's store, to the livery stable.

They have more business in the winter, when cars have trouble. In the summer, sometimes a traveling salesman will come in on the train, stay at the Phoenix Hotel, and hire a rig to visit customers in the area. Sometimes people in town want to hire a horse and buggy for a while just to go riding. A young man may hire one to take a girlfriend for a ride or go to a church social and then take someone home. People also like to ride horseback sometimes, just for the fun of it. That is what I would like.

The livery stable only has about half a dozen horses in the barn now. I don't know the name of the man who was cleaning out the stalls, but he was friendly. Baldy and I looked at all the horses and the buggies, saddles, and a sleigh (or cutter) and then went west on Main Street to Mr. Clark's blacksmith shop.

He is a big man with very strong arms. All blacksmiths have strong arms and shoulders from handling iron all day long. He is friendly to kids. He and his family live on Lena Street not far from Woody and they have a daughter, Esther. She is about the same age we are and is very pretty. He asked, "What can I do for you boys? Or are you just looking around?"

I said, "We are looking around, but what are you making?"

He said, "Oh, a farmer wants a heavy maul, for splitting chunks of wood. I thought I'd see if I could make an extra good one. They have to be about ten or twelve pounds, with a fairly long wedge and a hole big enough for a strong hickory handle." He had a piece of steel nearly ready. He heated it red hot, then put it on the anvil and hammered it to make the wedge really even on both sides. Then he put it in water, heated it, pounded it some more and repeated until he was satisfied. Then he tempered it some more and said, "Now it will hold an edge, but it doesn't have to be as sharp as an ax." We said it looked great to us. It was about noon. We went back to Dr. Tucker's office and soon Woody came out.

He did not look bad and he said he was all right. He said, "I had two fillings, but he didn't have to grind too much. I'm glad it's over." We split up to go home for dinner. This afternoon Woody came back in regular clothes. We rode over to Baldy's house on Oak Street. Then all of us rode out to Mr. Charlie Shoesmith's farm. It is on the edge of town and he doesn't care if we go there to play or look around.

We left our bikes in the barnyard then walked down to the creek and looked for animal tracks in the mud. We found some that looked like a racoon's and others made by dogs and cats and plenty of bird and mouse tracks.

After a while we went back to the barn, watched the animals a while, then went in the barn. We played in the haymow and in a separate part of the barn on the west side. That was like a shed and it was nearly full of nice-looking, small cardboard boxes. In each box, just like in a store, was a thing that had two halves that moved forward and backward when we pushed the handles. At the front end it was like a knitting needle. Mr. Shoesmith said it was an invention to help a person knit or weave. He did not say why he had so many of them, but he gave each of us one. It is interesting. Maybe I will learn how to use it.

We rode home in time for supper. It was really a great day.

JOSEPH HAD
A COAT

It was a little windy today, but sunny and really warm for spring. Coming back from Sunday school I rode my bike as fast as I could downhill from the depot to our house. I had my cap on with the bill toward the back so it would not blow off and the wind felt good in my face. I was wearing my best shirt and knickers, but riding didn't hurt them any. My long black stockings came up to my knees and the knickers came over my knees to make it neat and I wore my new leather dress shoes that lace up. They did not get scuffed either. Mother seems to worry about that when I get a new pair of shoes. For Sunday I was wearing a real four-in-hand necktie, a pretty blue one that flew out in back of me when I rode fast. My shirt was white, but my cap, knickers and shoes were brown. Of course, I rode my bike to Sunday school, too, but it was a lot slower going up hill. Our church is across the tracks about as far south as we live north on the same street.

Miss Lutz is our teacher for a class of boys, all of us about the same age. We don't all get to Sunday school every time, but usually there are four or five and sometimes maybe ten. Her first name is Margaret and her father, Mr. William Lutz, is a jeweler and also helps take care of the school. Her mother, Mrs. Chrissie Lutz, is on the school board and all of them are very important in the church. We like her because she is kind and patient and smiles and she always knows something interesting about the Bible. Most of it, if I try to read it myself, is hard to read and not very interesting, but when she tells stories or reads from the Sunday school book it seems like she is telling about real people.

This morning the lesson was about Joseph, the son of Jacob, who lived in the land of Canaan a long time ago. It must have been almost at the beginning of people because the story is in the Book of Genesis which is the first book in the Bible. Joseph was one of twelve sons of Jacob and he probably was kind of a tease or a smarty because his brothers did not like him very much. He told them he dreamed that he was going to be a ruler and they would have to bow down to him. They did not like that. So when he came out to see them while they were tending the sheep, they decided to kill him. One brother said not to kill him but to put him in a deep pit.

Joseph had a beautiful coat of many colors that his father had given him because he was the favorite. He was very proud of this coat and he was wearing it when he went out to see how his brothers were getting along with the sheep. They took away his coat before they put him in the pit. Some people from Gilead came along in a caravan and they bought Joseph for a slave and took him to Egypt. His brothers put goat blood on the coat of many colors and took it back to their father. Jacob thought wild animals had killed Joseph and he was very sad.

Many years later Joseph became an overseer of Egypt for the pharaoh. In a great famine his brothers came down to buy grain from Egypt because Joseph had made the Egyptians save up a lot of it. He was in charge and he sold his brothers the grain but gave them back the money and gave them a hard time because they did not know who he was. Finally, all his family came down to Goshen in Egypt and lived there through the famine and long afterward. Joseph and his brothers started the twelve tribes of Israel.

Mother took Virginia and Margery to church in the car, but she said I did not have to stay. As soon as I got home I changed into clothes I could be outdoors and play in. Then I rode my bike down to the Camp Ground to walk around the trees and look at the buttercups and May flowers and climb over the fences. Pretty soon I came back home. Mother and the girls were there. Ma said, "Daddy will be home soon. It is so nice, we will have Sunday dinner outdoors."

I helped carry the kitchen table and some chairs out to a place between the pump and the sandpile, partly under an apple tree, and then carried out plates, napkins, knives, forks, spoons and glasses of lemonade. Mother had made potato salad before and she was frying chicken. She opened some pickled beets she had canned and brought out some apple jelly for the hot biscuits.

Dad had been at the office to see some sick people. As soon as he came, he took off his straw hat and his bow tie and rolled up his shirt sleeves to come out with us.

It was a wonderful backyard picnic. Dad asked the blessing just like indoors and we were all happy and laughing. I felt sorry for Joseph and was glad I did not have any brothers to do mean things to me. He did get to be a ruler in Egypt, though, and got back at them. I wonder if his dad ever had his coat of many colors cleaned?

FOURTH OF JULY

My head really hurts, especially the right side. My jaw aches and it is hard to chew. A couple of days ago it was the Fourth of July. That is the birthday of our country and we really celebrated it.

In our backyard there is a big sandpile. My dad laid two-by-six-inch boards on their edges and fastened them with stakes to make a twelve-foot frame around a place that was nearly level. Then he had the lumberyard send a wagon with a lot of sand and dump it there. It made a great big sandpile. My sisters play in it, but sometimes my friends and I do, too.

We like to make roads and build big castles and walls and hills and valleys. It is more fun to do this when it is near the Fourth of July, because then we have many firecrackers. What we do is wet up the sand and build a big castle with towers and a moat and walls. Then we put firecrackers in various places in the castle towers and walls and blow them up. It is fun. We use up lots of matches and firecrackers.

Several of the fellows—Baldy and Woody and Aaron and Virgene and others, off and on—came the last few days and we built things and blew them up.

We also had torpedoes, but we had to throw them down hard on the sidewalk to make them explode.

Dad got some sacks of fireworks. On the evening of the Fourth of July, he waited till it was really dark, then he fired them off. He let me help. We drove some tall stakes in the ground beforehand. When the time came and some of our neighbors and friends were there, we fastened pinwheels on the stakes with nails. We lighted them and they turned round and round and made circles of fire. He let me hold a Roman candle and I was careful to aim it away from everybody. It kept shooting out little balls of fire time after time till it burned out. He let my friends hold them, too, and everybody was careful.

There were other fiery pieces that we nailed on the stakes, but they did not turn around. They just made pretty patterns. I guess the sky rockets were the most fun. Dad had made a trough about four feet long out of two boards. He put one end on the ground and the other end up so it pointed toward the sky out over the pasture north of us. He put a skyrocket in the trough with its stick toward the ground and its point toward the sky. Then he lit it and it made a whoosh of fire before it took off. It made a high arc in the air and when it burned out, the stick and burned papers fell in the pasture.

There were a good many skyrockets and soon he let me and my friends light them. Most of them went up all right, but a few just went up a little way then scooted along in the grass till they burned out. All the time we were shooting off firecrackers, mostly little ones, but a few big ones that made more noise.

Dad enjoyed it. Mother watched and tried to be sure nobody got hurt. My little sister Margery liked the lights but she did not like all the noise. Virginia wasn't sure how much she liked it. There are little lumps of material that come in a box and they are called snakes because when you light a match to one it "grows" out into a sort of wiggly worm or snake. Virginia found a box and got it open. She did not know what they were, so she ate one or two. Mother found her and thought they might be poison. She called Dad and he came and made her throw up. After that she was all right, but she was not really happy with fireworks.

After we had used up our skyrockets and sparklers and the other things, Mother gave everybody lemonade. We thought it was a good birthday party for our country.

Yesterday, Ellsworth (Alex) came over. We were talking about the Fourth of July and I had a few torpedoes left so we were throwing them on the sidewalk in front of our house to make them explode. Each one was round and long like a little sausage. One did not go off even though we threw it down several times. I got a hammer and pounded on it, but still it did not explode.

We wondered what was inside the torpedo to make it work, but the paper was so tough we could not tear it open with our hands. So I put it in my mouth and tried to chew on it with my right teeth to loosen it up. Just then it exploded. The noise was so loud I couldn't hear anything else for a while. It blew my jaw down and my mouth open hard, as if someone had hit me. Pretty soon I could tell that my throat was burned and there were little stones in my mouth along with pieces of paper. It really hurt. I suppose I hollered.

Alex ran up the hill and my mother came out of the house. When she saw what had happened she took me in the house to wash out my mouth and call Dad. There wasn't much blood, but there were many little stones to wash out. Dad examined me and decided there were not any broken bones or teeth. I could hear again, too. He said something about being lucky and that I should not do that again. I had sort of figured that out.

So that is why my head hurts after the Fourth of July.

UNCLE DAN REED

This morning, early, I walked over to Uncle Dan Reed's barn to watch him milk. He lives by the Camp Grounds, so it is just a few blocks away. It is in town, but he has a barn and cows and cats, just like on a farm. His house is on the side of the road next to the Camp Grounds and his barn is on the other side of the road. It is fun to visit him because he is friendly and has a big mustache. He doesn't trim it off short and neat like my dad's. It is big and bushy and he calls it his "handlebar" mustache. He is proud of it, I think, and takes good care of it. He smiles quite a bit and likes kids, but he doesn't have any of his own. He has a nice wife, but she is quiet and stays in the house. I don't see her very much.

Uncle Dan isn't my uncle, but all of us boys who go over to watch him milk or see his museum call him Uncle because he is good to us. Today he was really happy. The veterinarian, Dr. Yeager, had done tests on his cows to see if they had tuberculosis. He had just found out that they were all right. He said, "I knew they were fat and healthy, but I couldn't help worrying till I found out for sure." His cows are mostly

Brown Swiss, he says, but one is a Jersey like those my Uncle Otto in Indiana has. Each cow has her own stall. All eight of them go in just like trained pets and start eating the hay in their mangers. They were out in the pasture eating, but I guess they eat most of the time.

They stand there with their heads toward the inside of the barn and their hind legs almost outside. He has the barn opened up as much as he can because it is so warm. When they are settled in their stalls, he washes their udders with soap and water. The udder is a big bag back between the hind legs. It holds the milk and it has four long nipples that Uncle Dan gets milk out of. There are lots of flies. Uncle Dan tries to shoo them away and the cows switch their tails around to scare off the flies, too. When he is milking a cow he does not want her tail swinging around the milk pail, so he ties it to a big stone or a brick while he is working on her.

He talks to the cow and sits down on a stool and puts his head against her side, and then he takes one of the long nipples in each hand. He is a big man, but he is gentle with the cows. He said he doesn't want to hurt her, and if he did she probably wouldn't give down her milk. He showed me how to do it by squeezing with the fingers one after another so as to make the milk squirt out. If a person squeezed all the fingers at once, nothing would come out. I can't hardly get any milk, but he does it fast and gets a good stream, first from one nipple then another. Usually there is a cat sitting close by and every once in a while Uncle Dan squirts milk at the cat's face.

Then the cat opens his mouth and takes in the milk. They have done it lots of times and they like it.

As soon as Uncle Dan gets a pail about full, he carries it over to the watering trough and pours the milk into the big can sitting in the cool water. All the warm milk goes into the big milk cans to be cooled. The barn is about as clean as a barn can be, but that is not very clean. Mrs. Reed washes and scalds out all the pails and cans that hold milk and they have lids on to keep flies out.

All the customers have small tin milk cans of their own. They keep them clean and have their names on them. When the milk is cool, Uncle Dan fills the customers' cans and puts them in his Model T touring car. When the cows are through eating he turns them out to pasture.

Then he washes up again and gets in his car to deliver the milk. When I or some of my friends go along we ride in the front seat with him, and whenever he stops at somebody's house we pick the right can of milk or he gives it to us and we carry it to the house. Usually the lady is right there to take it. When we are not along, he does it all himself. The cows have to be milked twice a day, so he does the whole thing morning and evening.

Sometimes, after he has delivered the milk and finished the chores, he lets us go in his museum. This is a part of a big shed that he has cleaned. He has lots of things on the walls and in cases and on tables. There are many guns. One of them is from the Revolutionary War and it is called a Brown Bess. Some of the others are from the Civil War and Indian Wars and some are old muskets for hunting. He has sabers and bayonets and swords and knives. One is a doctor's knife, or lancet, that was used a long time ago to make sick people bleed so as to get rid of "bad blood." I'm glad they don't do that any more. He has many old-time farming tools and utensils and arrowheads. He even has some maps which he calls "plats" of the town of Davis from when it was first planned to be a town. He has a big drawing of a prison in the Civil War. It is called Andersonville and a lot of soldiers died there. He has army badges and medals from countries in Europe. They are all labeled to tell where they came from, but most of his things are not marked and he just tells about them. He likes to collect things for his museum. I think it would be fun, too. I'm glad he shows things to me and tells me about them.

He gave me a few things to start my museum. Two are cases, like picture frames, with military insignia in them. They are from European armies. Another thing I like is called a "flail." It is made of a long piece of wood tied loosely at the end to a shorter, heavier piece of wood at its end. A man uses the long stick as a handle and swings it so the heavy stick hits piles of cut wheat on the ground. The flail knocks the ripe heads off the wheat. Then the farmer tosses the wheat in the air a little so the wind can blow the chaff away. It is an old-fashioned way to thresh.

From Uncle Dan's, I cut across the Schermerhorn place to go to Woody's house. The Schermerhorn house is real old. At first it was an inn where stagecoaches stopped and people going from Chicago to Galena could eat or stay overnight. It is made out of stone. I suppose it looks about the same now as when it was an inn. They say Abraham Lincoln stayed there when he was a lawyer, before he was president.

Woody was practicing his clarinet. I listened for a while and it reminded me that I had to practice my cornet. I haven't hardly played it since my last lesson. Mr. Sprague won't like that very much. So I came home to practice it a little.

THE ROCKS

There is a place out east of Lena toward Damascus that people call The Rocks. It is a valley with a good creek flowing through it twisty-like. The valley is not very wide, and on each side of it are wooded hills and big rocks. Some of the rocks are like boulders, every which way on the hills. A couple are like huge towers on the edge of a hill. We can get up on top and there is room to walk around a little or to build a small picnic fire for roasting weenies and marshmallows. This part of the valley is about half a mile long. Beyond that, either way, it opens out to pasture land. Actually, cows go in the rough part, too, but I don't think they like the hills and rocks and thistles and trees as well as the open grassy pastures.

This afternoon was warm and sunny. Baldy came by on his bike and asked if I wanted to go out to The Rocks. He had his air rifle. I said, "Sure," then asked Ma if it was all right. She said it was, and to be careful, and would we like peanut butter and jelly sandwiches. We waited while she made the sandwiches, wrapped them in oiled paper and put them in a paper sack. I filled my second-hand army canteen with water from the pump, got my Daisy rifle, put a leather poke full of BB's in my pocket and was ready to go. I have a knapsack, but it was too hot a day to wear that. I just put stuff in the basket of my bike.

We rode out of town east on Lena Street past Woody's house. We asked him if he wanted to go along, but he said not this time, he had something else to do. He has been out there lots of times, of course. At the edge of town we turned left on the Townline Road. It goes to Cedarville, ten miles away, but The Rocks is only two miles. The road is gravel and dusty. Not many cars use it, so most of the dust that came up around us was what we made ourselves. When we came to the valley of The Rocks, the road went down on rocky ledges almost like stair steps. We walked the bikes part of the way. It is really rough for cars. After we crossed the bridge and got to the other side of the valley, we came to the gate, opened it, brought our bikes in and closed the gate again. Whenever we go through any farm gates we are very careful to close them. My dad said it makes a farmer mad to leave his gates open.

We hiked in carrying our stuff. We had already drunk part of the water on the way out, but it did not matter because there is a spring full of cool fresh water at the north end of The Rocks. Watercress grows there and it is boxed in so the cows cannot mess it up. Sometimes bullfrogs get in.

It was so shady and breezy and peaceful there; it was wonderful. We walked around the tall Canadian thistles and watched out for fallen logs and garter snakes and cow pies. Some of the time we walked in the stream because it felt good. Our tennis shoes kept the sharp stones from hurting our feet and it was easier to stand up. There are lots of little fishes in the deeper pools of the creek and plenty of frogs, crayfish, dragonflies and other bugs. Most of them did not bother us, but horseflies, sweatbees, mosquitos and little black no-see-um bugs like to bite.

We came to a bend in the creek where it made a deep pool by a slanted rock near a cliff. It was very cool and dark with shade. We sat down on the grass to enjoy it and then we decided we were hungry. It was a good time to eat our sandwiches. They were really delicious. We ate every bit and then put the sack and oiled paper under a stone before we climbed up to the top of the big rock.

They say that a slab of stone was cut off the top of the big rock to make the monument in town which is a memorial to all the Lena soldiers who went to the Great War. The stone looks the same, so maybe that is where they got it. We walked up the hill and climbed up and down the big rock, and the other one that is nearly as big, several times, then hiked on toward the spring.

At the edge of the woods out on the pasture side we set up some targets to shoot at with our BB guns. Just like Dad taught us, we put the sticks and leaves and stones we were going to shoot at on the hillside so we were shooting into the hill. We had fun with that. Both of us are pretty good shots and can hit most anything we think is reasonable. When we walked across the flat land we saw gopher holes and groundhog holes, but we were not hunting for the animals. They are varmints and farmers are glad to get rid of them, but you can't kill them with BB guns.

When we got to the spring, it was a good time to rest again. So we drank spring water by putting our faces right down to it, and we filled my canteen for the trip home. We ate some watercress. It tastes bitter and sharp and stings a little. It is fun to eat.

While we loafed around there, we watched the yellow butterflies, white butterflies, pigeons, blue jays, redwing blackbirds, crows, Holstein cattle and lots of other things. When we were quiet, every once in a while a gopher or groundhog would sit up where we could see him. When a gopher is running around or ducks into a hole, if you whistle a strong high note he will sit up straight and listen.

The shadows were getting longer. We started home, but were not in a hurry because we liked it there so much. The creek wandered on the flat floor of the valley and we just followed right along its banks. There is one pond that is deep enough to swim in. Baldy and I do not know how to swim, but we took off our shirts and pants and waded real deep in our underwear. Everything got wet, but we sure didn't care. After a while we just stood out in the sunshine and dried off.

Finally we got back to our bikes. We hated to leave, but we did not want to miss supper either. So we walked our bikes up the rough, stony road until we came to the level part and then rode back to town. We split where Townline Road meets Lena Street. He stayed on the road to cross the railroad and go to his house on the south side of town while I went on Lena Street to old Mr. Harbach's house then down hill to home.

Mother asked how it had been. That was a hard question to answer. I told her we had a dusty ride, we saw a lot of things and had a wonderful time. I didn't know how to tell her what it is like to spend a beautiful summer afternoon with a good friend.

THRESHING

Yesterday Waldo invited me out to his home. His mother and dad wanted me to come because they were harvesting wheat and had threshers. They thought it would be interesting and it certainly was. Waldo lives on a farm about two miles south of town, but he has aunts in Lena and visits them often. His family also goes to church in town. He knows all of us boys, even though we do not see him quite so often as we do one another. He is cheerful and friendly. Everybody calls him Happy or Hap.

It was sunny and hot. I wore my overalls and a straw hat and rode my bike to their farm. I thought it was fairly early in the morning, but they had been working a long time. Threshers are other farmers from nearby farms. They like to get as much done in a day as they can so as to get the wheat in the grain bins and granaries before the weather changes. When I rode over the hill just before reaching their house, I could hear the clanking and see the smoke of the steam powered engine and threshing machine. They used tractors and horse teams to bring in wagon loads of golden wheat to be separated into grain and straw.

The straw is put into stacks and sometimes bales for storage and then used for bedding for animals. The grain is used for food, like flour and Shredded Wheat.

When I got down to the threshing place between the house and barn I found Happy. He smiled and said, "Hi," then told me to lean my bike against a tree and come around with him. He showed me the big black steam engine with its coal and wood burning furnace and big boiler and smoke stack, and steam blowing out at the sides. It had a big fly-wheel on one side and a long belt went from the drive wheel on the other side to the threshing machine to give it power. It knocks the heads off the wheat, saves the grain, blows the straw to a pile and blows away the little pieces or chaff like dust.

Happy and I carried water and lemonade to the men and sometimes brought tools or messages back and forth. He said he could drive a team but they didn't need him to do it then.

Happy's dad was looking after everything, checking the machines, keeping the wagons moving, telling people where to put things and so on. He was cheerful and happy that he had lots of wheat and that he had been able to cut it, bundle it, stack it in shocks, and now thresh it without a big rainstorm spoiling it. He asked if I wanted to go out to the field. I said, "Sure," and climbed up on a wagon with him. One of his friends was driving the tractor pulling the wagon and we went bumpity-bump out to the big field where the piles of wheat were waiting to be loaded. Each pile was made up of a few tied sheaves of wheat piled upright together and then one bundle over the top as a cap. That one would help shed water if it rained before threshing time. I could see that the fields were nearly cleared. The men agreed they could finish by the end of the afternoon. I rode the wagon around and helped fill it. When we reached the threshing machine again I jumped off. Happy said his mother wanted us in the house.

The wives of the men in the threshing ring were fixing dinner. The men always like to eat a great deal at threshing time. They work hard and sweat and have big appetites. The ladies like to get together and cook big dinners. Everybody has fun along with the hard work. When people talk about "eating like a thresher," they mean really eating a great deal. The ladies have worked together for years and they plan it ahead.

The house was not big enough for people to come inside to eat. Happy and I carried saw horses and planks from a shed to make a table under a big maple tree. His mother put sheets over them for a cover. We brought out plates, knives, forks, spoons and cups to help hold the table cloths down. We also brought out chairs, but if there were not enough a person could always take his plate and things and go sit on a wagon or somewhere else. We helped carry big serving kettles and dishes out to the table and there were large bowls and jugs of lemonade and water. When dinner was nearly ready, Happy and I went out and yelled at the men and his mother rang a bell.

The men were hot and hungry. They had been looking forward to the dinner. At the signal they stopped what they were doing and went to the pump to wash up and splash water on themselves wherever it felt good. Then they picked up plates and cups to fill. There was fried chicken, chicken and dumplings, sausage, ham, mashed potatoes, gravy, scalloped potatoes, baked beans, green beans, peas, beets, lettuce, carrots, onions, pickles, potato salad, bread, butter, jelly, jam and several pies and cakes. I know I can't remember it all. It looked like enough for an army. Some sat at the table, others at different places, but everybody paid attention to eating. Everything was delicious. I was hungry, too, and I ate my share.

As they were getting ready to go back to work, everyone said how good it was and that every year it got better. Soon all the men and machines were going full swing and the wagons full of new wheat were heading for the granary. I stayed till about five o' clock. Happy said they would be finished before long. I was supposed to be home by six. I did not think I would be able to eat supper. I thanked Happy and his folks for a wonderful time and a great dinner.

The bicycle ride home built up my appetite, I guess. When I coasted up to our pump I tried to wash off some of the dirt and chaff before going in the house. Mother said, "You look as if you had a good day. Are you ready for supper?" I said, "I ate so much this noon, I shouldn't be hungry, but I am." So I went in and had a nice fried steak and fried potatoes supper Ma had fixed. I drank at least three glasses of milk. My sisters thought I was a mess. I was tired and happy.

PAL AND
THE GROUNDHOG

Boy, am I tired and hot! I almost wish it was time to have a bath, but it will be a couple of days yet before Ma sets that old washtub out on the kitchen floor and half-fills it with water. She puts cold water in then warms it up with water from the tea kettle. Then she lays out the soap and wash rag and towel and tells me to take a bath and she goes into the dining room. I am almost too big to really sit down in the tub but I can stand in it and double up real tight to sit in it a little and use the wash cloth to get all over. It feels good to get all cleaned up again. Tonight I'll take a stand-up bath with a wash rag.

Anyway, this afternoon Baldy came over. He was wearing his blue shirt, work pants and tennis shoes. He had his hunting knife in its leather sheath on his belt. I had my overalls on and my jack knife in my pocket. He said, "Hey, Vic, let's hike up to High Point."

I said, "O.K., I'll ask Ma."

She said that would be fine and made each of us a sandwich of cold boiled ham, with mustard on the bread. She wrapped them in oiled paper and said,

"Now you won't starve before you get home." We carried them in our pockets like everything else. Pal seemed to get the idea that we were going to do something. He was jumping around and sniffing. Maybe he liked the smell of the sandwiches. Like all beagles, Pal likes to hunt and he wanted to go with us. We were glad to have him.

First we cut across the back of Downing's lot to the big barn where Mr. Downing packs ice. It has lots of wet sawdust in it now but not much ice left. In the winter he cuts ice out at the pond west of town and puts it in sawdust in the barn, and then he covers it all with more sawdust so the ice does not melt for a long time. We walked in the wet sawdust and looked for ice but there wasn't much to see, so we went west on Lena Street. Most of our streets don't have names, or at least I do not know what they are, but Lena Street is the main one going east and west on the north side of town. It goes to Freeport if you go east and to Galena if you go west far enough.

The road is dirt with gravel on top and we kicked up dust as we walked. We passed a small stone house, then the Catholic Church and then, at the edge of town, was the little wooden house where Ray lives, but he was not home. Downhill and over to the right was the pond. It is an old gravel pit now filled with water. We walked down to it and took our shoes and socks off to wade. We stayed near the edge because they say it is deep in the middle and we don't know how to swim. Pal swims though. He would jump right in to get sticks we threw out for him.

Just a little way further west is a place called
Boyer's Woods. There is a clearing in it where we
kids sometimes have picnics. We tried to run around
in the woods but there was so much underbrush we
could not go very fast. We went down the road again
to a little creek then started the long hike up the big
hill to High Point.

Pretty soon we came to a farm house at five
corners. Roads go off in five directions from there
and the place is called Louisa. It used to be a little
town, I guess, but now it just has a cemetery at the
southwest and the big old Brethren Church on the
north. It has been there a long time and many people
go to church there. Our friend Art Wagner goes
because his dad is the preacher. This summer they
had Daily Vacation Bible School and Baldy and I
went because of Art. Baldy belongs to the Lutheran
Church and I go to the Methodist Church, but we
both thought it was fun to attend the Brethren Bible
School. They have a pump out in front. Pal, Baldy
and I walked over to get a drink. It was hard to get
the pump started and the water was a little rusty at
first, but soon it was cold and clear and tasted good.
We used the tin cup that hung on the pump. It was
rusty, too, but we washed it out. We let Pal have
some water out of the cup, but he got most of his
from the puddles we made around the pump.

From there on up it was sort of steep. Most cars
have to shift gears or go into low to get up the hill,
and that was what we did, too. We just walked and
did not say much, but did not stop to rest till we
reached a farm near the top. It was the Reynold's
place, I think. We didn't go in but just caught our

breath for a while. Then we went the rest of the way up the hill. The road goes along on the shoulder of the hill pretty high, but to get to the real top we left the road and crawled through the fence to the pasture just north.

The top of High Point is about as high as you can get in Illinois. My dad said there is a hill about twenty-five miles west of here called Charles Mound that is a few feet higher, but it is an Indian mound. High Point is a real hill, with oak trees on top and some pits that have been dug in the ground. Some people say these are prospector holes dug a long time ago when the pioneers were looking for lead to mine, like what they found at Galena.

It was great to be as high as we could get on the hill. The wind was cool and there was shade under the trees. Part way down the hill were thorn apple trees with tiny little green apples growing on them. We were hungry so we sat down in the shade and took out our sandwiches. They were mashed out of shape, but they sure tasted good. Pal said he was hungry, too. We each gave him a couple of bites.

While we sat under the oak trees we just rested and looked out across the valley to hills a long way away. In the valley was a little stream called Waddams Creek. It is named after the man who brought his family and settled right near this hill a long time ago. He was the first white man who stayed here. He and his family were pioneers. Before that there were Indians here.

Baldy said, "I wonder what it was like when the Americans came in here and had to fight the Indians?

Mr. Eells said soldiers chased the Indians right down this valley."

"Sure," I told him, "they had a battle over there about as far as we can see. And Mr. Eells said the big battle was as far as we can see the other way at Kellog Grove."

"That was the Black Hawk War," Baldy said. "I'll bet it was exciting, riding horses and chasing Indians. There weren't any roads, either. They rode through the high grass and the trees and I bet they hollered and yelled."

"They shot their guns, too," I said. "Three soldiers and an Indian were killed over there where Captain Stephenson caught up with the Indians. Mr. Eells knows all about it."

After we got tired of resting we walked over to where we could look south across the road and across the wide valley to the next ridge. That is where Kellog Grove is and where the settlers and soldiers fought the Indians a long time ago.

All of a sudden we heard Pal barking like he was all excited and it was important.

We ran over to him. He was facing a big old groundhog. He must have caught him away from his den, because usually a groundhog or woodchuck would just run into his hole in the ground. When this one saw us, he turned and climbed up the oak tree nearby. He went out on a limb and looked down at us. He was angry and making noise with his teeth and probably scared, too. We wanted to get him because groundhogs make bad holes in fields and pastures and sometimes horses and cows step in them and hurt or break their legs. Groundhogs and gophers are called varmints and everybody tries to get rid of them because they make trouble for farmers.

For a while we looked at the groundhog and he looked at us and Pal barked with his neck and back hair all standing up. We could tell he really wanted to get at the groundhog.

Baldy said, "I'll climb up and shake him down. You and Pal get him." He managed to climb up the tree to the right limb. Then he shook it real hard. The groundhog held on. He shook it more and more. Finally the groundhog fell off. He landed near Pal and got on his feet snarling and gnashing his teeth. Pal made the quickest move I ever saw him make. He grabbed the groundhog by the throat with his teeth and started shaking him. I had my knife in hand and Baldy came down and got his knife out, but neither of us could get hold of the groundhog. They growled and snarled something awful. Pal choked and shook him to death. When the groundhog was quiet, Pal was panting and wagging his tail We petted him and told him what a good dog he was. Gradually his hair laid down. He is a hunting dog and he did what he was supposed to do. The groundhog was about the same size as he was. If the groundhog had got hold of Pal he would have hurt him real bad.

Well, it was exciting. Now we were on High Point with a groundhog to carry home. We took turns carrying him by the tail, but it was a long hike home. We told Mother all about it. She did not say much, but she did not seem as excited about it as we were. When Dad came home for supper, he said it was all right, but maybe lucky none of us got bit. He showed us how to skin the groundhog so we could have its hide. Then we tacked the hide on a board with the fur toward the wood and rubbed salt into the other side of the skin. Now it will dry without rotting.

Baldy stayed for supper after Ma called his folks and they said it was all right. We were really hungry. There was round steak that Mother had pounded and then fried, fried potatoes, lots of good cold milk from Uncle Dan's brown Swiss cows and, what do you know, a cherry pie Mother had baked. We ate all we could hold and Pal was happy with the scraps. I think he was really proud of himself the way he had stood up to that old groundhog.

ANDY AND
THE AIRPLANE

Andy is taller than I am and I guess a little older. We are both pretty skinny and we are in the same grade at school. Andy doesn't always learn as fast as the rest of the kids, but he is better than anyone at making things and doing things with his hands. He knows a lot about machines and even airplanes. He can hammer and saw and cut wood and whittle better than I can.

Two times this summer a pilot brought his airplane to Lena to take people for rides in it. They call that barnstorming and some men make money that way. They charge five dollars for a ride in the airplane.

Andy and I didn't have five dollars for a ride, but we were all excited about seeing an airplane up close. So each time the plane came, we walked across town to a big pasture near Mr. Shoesmith's house and watched. That is on Oak Street Road, out from where we lived when we first came here.

The first time, we saw the airplane in the sky just about when he said it would come. The pilot had sent handbills on ahead and some of my friends

had helped pass them out all over town. He came
down close and swooped over the pasture to see what
it was like. Then he went back up in the air and circled
just above the houses so everyone would know he
was there. He returned and landed just as nice as
you please.

The airplane was big and had two wings and a
tail, a long body with an engine and wooden propeller
in front. The pilot sat in a little well or cockpit in
the body. He called the body the fuselage. There was
a little windshield in front of him, but no cover over
him. So he wore goggles and a helmet. I asked him
if it wasn't awfully cold and windy up high in the
sky. He said, "No, it isn't bad. It's a lot of fun."

By this time some people had driven up to see
the airplane and a man with a gasoline truck had
come out to put some gas in the airplane's tank. Pretty
soon several people had paid their money for rides
and they stood in a special area. He took them up
one at a time. He gave them a helmet and goggles
to wear, helped them get in the second cockpit, then
he got settled in the first one and made a sign to
the man with the gasoline truck. That man then went
over and pulled down on one side of the propeller
to start the engine. It started right away and made
a lot of noise as the pilot accelerated to see if it was
working all right. The propeller made a big wind
behind it. We ran back to feel it blow on us. It made
our hair go back and was fun. But it also blew dirt
and stuff. So we returned to where the other people
were.

The airplane started off real slow, then went faster and faster up the sloping pasture. When he got near the fence he made a horseshoe turn and came back going faster all the time. Finally the plane lifted off the ground and went up high enough to go over some trees and on up into the sky. We yelled and clapped our hands.

The pilot took each passenger for about a five minute ride. Each time he came down from the side toward town, making nice landings so the wheels and the tail skid hit the ground at the same time. He called that his three point landing and was very proud of it. The passengers were happy and excited and they said the landings did not shake them up at all. They liked to be up in the sky and look down at the town and all the things they knew. They said it was fun to look a long way out and to see the clouds up close.

He made lots of trips. There were still some people who would have liked to go, but he said he had to get somewhere before dark and he had to leave. He said he would come back in a few weeks and take everyone who couldn't go up this time.

Later he did come back and Andy and I went over to see him again. It was about the same, but we did not get tired of watching the airplane speed up its motor and wobble off to a slow start, then go faster and faster in its big horseshoe take-off into the sky like a great big bird. It must be wonderful to feel free as a bird flying in the sky. Everybody got excited about it.

Just now—it has been a couple of weeks since the pilot was here—Andy brought me a present. It is a model airplane, a little airplane which looks just like the big one. It has a fuselage which he whittled out of a small log and two wings he made out of boards. He whittled a propeller for it and on top of where the engine would be he put a sparkplug nut as the opening for water to cool the engine. It has a nice big tail, wheels and tail skid, and a cockpit. It is just dandy and I thanked him. I will always keep it.

THE MONTAGUE PLACE

Yesterday was all rainy. I stayed inside most of the time. When I took Pal out for a little while, Mother said, "Be sure to wipe your feet when you come in." I scuffed mine back and forth on the mat, but Pal didn't. I walked him around in the screened porch before he went in the rest of the house.

I spent a good deal of time reading a Roy Blakeley book. It is a good book. The boys in it are Boy Scouts and they have fun and adventures. Pretty soon I will be old enough to be a Lone Scout and I will join. We do not have a Scout troop here.

Today it is bright sunny summer again. Most everything dried off this morning. Right after noon I called Baldy and Woody and Aaron and asked them if they would like to go out to the Montague Place. Mother said we could take food for a picnic supper if we wanted to. They all said, "Sure." They rode their bikes to our place and leaned them against the trees and house while Ma got our food ready.

Woody pumped while I filled my canteen with water. Ma put some lemonade in a thermos jar and then she put some dried beef and jelly sandwiches and some butter and brown sugar sandwiches on the counter of the kitchen cabinet. She gave us some pickles and olives and an apple apiece. Then the best of all, she gave us two cans of Vienna sausages. I ran up to my room to get my Sterno canned heat stove and some matches and put my hunting knife on my belt.

Then we divided up everything and wrapped whatever needed it in oil paper. Mother gave us paper sacks to pack things in, each of us put his share in his bike basket and we took off. Pal ran right along. He likes to go with us all the time. When we are not busy, he chases rabbits and squirrels and cats. He doesn't catch anything, though.

We rode west on Lena Street way out to Louisa then turned north on Five Points Road. It goes right up a hill. About half way up we stopped to rest and take a swig of water. Riding a bike up hill is hot in the summer. We kept going and after a while we crossed Waddams Creek and then came to Pin Hook Road where we turned.

About a quarter of a mile down Pin Hook we came to the Montague house on the north side of the road. It is a nice old stone house built from blocks of stone which they cut in a quarry near here. Mr. Eells knows all about these things and he said the house was built over seventy-five years ago and was a great mansion for pioneers. Mr. Montague and his family had a big orchard and also a regular farm. It had pretty gardens and everything. It is sort of run-down now, but it is still neat to see it and think about the way it used to be. Along the road before we came to the house we saw the two big tall American chestnut trees that Mr. Eells says are the only ones left in this part of the country. All the rest were killed by some kind of tree disease thirty or forty years ago. He keeps trying to get new trees from these old ones, but so far he has not got one to grow. Something happens to the chestnuts.

Watching out for cows, we walked down to Waddams Creek on the south side of the road. We played around the creek and pasture for a while, then rode our bikes back up Pin Hook and down Five Points just a short way to a gate that let us in the pasture east from the Montague house. We sort of call the whole area the Montague Place, but maybe someone else owns it all now. We don't know why they call it Pin Hook Road. There is a school on it that is called Pin Hook School. Mr. Eells said some people think the children from the school sometimes fished in the creek with pins bent into hooks. Farther north is Indian Creek and that seems right because there were Indians here when Mr. Waddams brought his family in.

Anyway, we went in the pasture and walked our bikes over the hill to a nice level place near the creek. We were ready for some lemonade and a few olives. For quite a while we hiked along and in the creek and up and around the rocks and cliffs across it.

When we were good and hungry, we got out our picnic things. I used my Boy Scout knife to open the cans of Vienna sausages. they taste good cold, but I wanted to heat some of them on my Sterno stove. I don't get to use it very often. The canned heat lighted up right away and soon the little pan was hot. I heated the sausages then picked them up with sharp sticks

I had whittled and gave them to the guys. We ate everything. It was good.

We had seen everything we wanted to. The cows had not bothered us. Pal had been happy with his sausage. So we wadded everything but the thermos bottle and the canteen in one sack and put it all in my bike basket to take home.

It would have been a long ride home alone, but with friends it was not very long. When we split up to go to our own homes we all said, "So long. Let's do it again sometime."

COWBOYS AND RUSTLER

The day before yesterday it was hot and sunny and my dog, Pal, just wanted to lie there and pant. He is a good beagle and he likes to chase rabbits, but not now. It is a really hot summer. While I was sitting on the door step of the screened porch just back of our kitchen and drinking some great lemonade my Ma had just fixed, Baldy came up. He was wearing his cowboy hat and boots and overall pants, or Levi's as they call them out west. He had his rope lassoo and his gun holster with a cap pistol in it.

He said, "Let's play cowboy. Bet I can rope better than you." He could, too, but I wasn't going to let on.

I said, "Sure. Here, you finish the lemonade and I'll go get my stuff."

I had about the same kind of outfit he had. We both liked to read about the West and we played at it whenever we could.

Pretty soon I was back from my room all ready to be a cowboy. Pal got up and checked me out by sniffing at everything he could reach, but he wasn't very enthusiastic. He just went out to the backyard with us because he was tired of lying down and didn't have anything else to do.

Our backyard is big and has lots of trees of all sizes, maple, box elder, apple, cherry, and lots of bushes. It is fenced because Dad raises chickens as his hobby and there is a chicken house where the chickens and a few ducks live. They do not stay in the house very much in the daytime but spread out through the trees and enjoy the shade. The hens have their nests in the house and they lay eggs there, but the ducks like to make their own nests out at the far end of the lot, and sometimes they hatch out little ducklings there. We gather the hen eggs to eat, but we don't like the duck eggs very much, so we do not really care what the ducks do with them. The little ducklings are cute when they hatch.

There are a couple of old fence posts standing alone and some other things like tree limbs that we could use for roping practice. We galloped along pretending we were on horses, swinging the loops of our lariats around. Then we tried to throw the loop over a post or a tree stub. Sometimes we tried to rope Pal or a chicken or a duck, but we were not very good. We did better with the posts. I did lassoo Baldy, but that was just a joke.

After a while Virgene came over. She lives next door and is about the same age as we are. She was wearing nearly the same things we were, except she did not have a gun or a lariat. She could run and pretend she was on a horse and play Out West, too. She said she wanted to play cowboy with us. We said, "Sure," and Baldy said we would play cowboys and rustler.

I said, "You can be the rustler. We will pretend the chickens and ducks are our herd of cows. While we are asleep at night you come and steal some of them and when we find out about it we will chase you."

Baldy and I went around a corner of the chicken house that we called our ranch barn and lay down in the shade of a big old tree. It was so cool that we didn't care whether we chased a rustler or not. Soon the ducks started quacking real loud, so I said, "Baldy, some rustler must be getting after our cows."

Baldy said, "Yep, I recken yore right. We better catch 'em."

So we ran around the corner of the ranch barn and sure enough there was Virgene holding a big drake who was flapping one wing trying to get away. When she saw us she started to run, carrying the drake. She is a good runner and when she went around through the trees, we were not gaining on her. The big mallard got away so she could run better than ever. Baldy said, "You go that way and I'll go the other and head her off."

It worked because she turned to get away from him and I caught her. I had my rope ready and I dropped the loop over her head and arms and pulled it tight. Baldy came galloping up and he tied her hands behind her back. Then he said, "Now we've got you dead to rights, Rustler. We will have a trial. I'll be the sheriff and Vic will be the judge."

She said, "The cow got away. You don't have any evidence."

Baldy said, "It doesn't matter. We saw you take it. You are a rustler."

So I said, "I am going to sit on this box and it will be the judge's bench. This is the courtroom and the trial will begin. Sheriff, what did this prisoner do?"

Baldy said, "You are supposed to call the courtroom to order. Anyway, we saw this prisoner steal a cow. She is a rustler."

I said, "Rustler, what do you have to say for yourself?"

She said, "The cow got away. I don't think I'm a rustler anymore."

I said, "The sheriff saw you take it. You have to be taught a lesson. I sentence you to three months in jail and a one hundred dollar fine."

She said, "I don't have a hundred dollars."

He said, "I don't have a jail."

I said, "The sentence will be four months in jail and no fine. Sheriff, you can use the ranch barn for a jail."

He marched her to the chicken house, put her in and closed the door. It was hot in there. Right away she stuck her head out a window and said, "This jail smells bad. It smells like chickens. It is too hot."

Baldy was standing guard at the door. He said, "Prisoners always complain. Don't pay any attention, Judge."

All of us got tired of not doing anything. The sheriff said, "I'm tired of standing guard." The prisoner said, "Isn't it four months yet?"

I pretended to look at a calendar and then I said, "Well, what do you know, Sheriff, the prisoner's jail sentence is up and you can turn her loose."

Baldy said, "Now that you are not a rustler anymore, you can be a cowboy. Do you want to work on our ranch?"

Virgene said, "Yes. What do I do?" He said, "We will round up the cows and put them on the trail to market."

We pretended to ride our horses around slowly. We got nearly all the chickens and ducks in a group and walked them toward the end of our lot. They were always trying to go different directions. We headed them off and there was a lot of quacking and squawking. We pretended it was mooing and bawling. Finally we herded them to the fence. I said, "We have reached Abilene. This is the market and it is the end of the big drive. I will pay you off and you can look for new jobs." I pretended to give them money.

Baldy said, "Let's see if this ranch on the other side of the fence needs cowboys."

We climbed over the fence to Mr. Skene's pasture. There were several Holstein cows eating grass in the pasture. We did not try to herd them together, but we went up and patted them. They did not pay much attention to us. We could just barely hear Virgene's mother calling her home for supper. She said, "I guess the roundup is over. So long."

Baldy said, "I'd better go home, too. So long."

I said, "See you tomorrow." I walked home and sat on the kitchen steps to wait for supper.

I thought we would play cowboys and bank robbers the next day. But it was a little bit drizzly and several of the guys came over. It was a great day for a green apple fight.

DAD CALLS ME JACK

There were lots of green apples lying around and we got in some good throws. Some of us have real bruises. Virgene is about as good a shot as the guys.

BICYCLE TAG

Well, I really got my hands skinned up this time. And my chin, a little bit, and my cheek and my head hurts, too. Four of the guys came over this afternoon with their bikes. I got mine and we rode to the Camp Ground.

Camp Meeting is over now. The tents are gone but the big tabernacle and the regular buildings and the barn are always there. It is all cleaned up. What we like are the big trees and the nice long grass and all the birds and squirrels. We parked our bikes and walked and ran around among the trees and talked about when Indians were in woods like these, maybe right here.

We walked to the creek behind the Camp Grounds and went along it for a while. There isn't much water in it now. We can jump across it most everywhere. Baldy pushed Woody and made him get a foot wet, then Woody pushed Baldy and made him get both feet wet. Then we all walked in the creek and got all of our feet wet. It was fun.

We went back to our bikes and rode past our place up to Lena Street and west to the pond. There we hiked up to the big cliff on one side of the pond and looked over it and threw some rocks in it. We ran around the end of the pond to where there is a little muddy-grassy creek and got our feet wet again. It doesn't matter. It is so hot everything dries right away.

We rode back and I told the guys I had just thought up a game. We would go to our house and get some sofa pillows and two fellows would stand on each side of the sidewalk a way apart. Each one would have a pillow. Then the other one would ride his bike down the hill as fast as he could and go between them. They would throw their pillows at him. If they hit him, he would have to take a place in the standing-line and one of the pillow-throwers would take his turn riding the bike. If he didn't get hit, the one who was "It" would ride again. We would keep it up till everybody had a chance to ride or until we got tired of it.

Woody and Baldy thought it was a good idea and they said nobody could hit them. So maybe we should not let whoever was "It" take more than two rides before giving the next one a turn. Aaron wasn't sure his bike would go fast enough but he was willing to try. Barton said he would bet he could knock Baldy off his bike no matter how fast he was going.

We wheeled into our yard and jumped off our bikes just like cowboys swinging off their horses. I went in the house and got some pillows. Ma was busy and I think it was just as well she did not see me.

I gave each of the others a pillow then I rode up by old man Harbach's house, stopped, and turned back down the hill. They were lined up two in our yard and two between the big trees along the street, all facing the sidewalk. It was just like the Indians making someone run the gauntlet. I yelled, "Here I come," jumped on my bike and pumped it up as fast as I could. They yelled and threw the pillows as I flew by. The first two missed but one of the others hit me on the shoulder so I was tagged. It was exciting, though.

Each of the others rode in turn. One or two got through but usually the rider was tagged by a pillow. They all thought it was fun. It came to be my turn again and I thought to myself, "I will go so fast this time that nobody can tag me." At the starting place I aimed my bike down hill and yelled, "Wahooo" as I swung on and started. Well, I was going fast all right, and the first three pillows missed me. The last one missed me, too, but it hit the front wheel of my bike, caught in the spokes and the bike and I went up and over like a big pinwheel and down we came together on the sidewalk. I cannot quite figure it out, but I must have landed on my hands and head because that is where the scrapes and bumps are.

They pulled me loose from the bike and we all tried to see if anything was broken. Both the bicycle and I seemed all right except for where I was bleeding. The fellows helped me over to the pump and pumped water while I washed up. It really hurt and stung, even the water on my hands hurt and my head was starting to thump. After my hands stopped bleeding and they said I looked better, somebody said, "Maybe we ought to play something else." That was okay with me. So I shook the pillows carefully and took them back through the front door. Ma was working in the kitchen. She did not notice.

We set up an old box for a target and took turns throwing green apples at it to see who could knock it over the most times out of five throws. Baldy was the best, but the rest of us were not too bad. It sort of made me forget how much my hands and head hurt. Pretty soon it was getting toward supper time, so everybody said, "So long" and went home.

When I went in for supper, Ma looked at me and said, "What in the world happened to you?"

I said, "I fell off my bike."

CRAWLING
THROUGH THINGS

Today we spent all afternoon going through things. Virgene and Baldy came over and it was hot and dry. We didn't feel like doing much. For a while we just sat on the ground and the swing watching bugs and sparrows and the cat and dog. They were not doing much either. Pal, my beagle, stretched out on the ground and panted with his tongue hanging out. He kept an eye on Old Bill, the mostly-white cat who was lying in one of his favorite places, on the door sill of the barn. He was asleep, but every now and then he peeked out to check on Pal. They do not really fight, but there is always the feeling that they might if they got too close. Cactus, Dad's horse, was in the barn with his head over the box-stall looking out. The barn doors were open. There were lots of sparrows around the barn, but the cat was not bothering them. Sometimes he chases them, but they usually get away.

I said, "Let's go up in the haymow and make tunnels in the hay." Baldy said, "It's probably too hot but it's something to do." Virgene said, "Sure, why not?" We had done it before, but not for quite a while.

Our barn is not very big. There is only room for one good- sized box stall on the ground floor with enough space around it for a big oats box, a ladder going up to the haymow and a walkway around two sides of the stall. When we came here the barn was used for a garage. There was not any stall or oats box or hay. I remember one day when Mother accidentally drove the car forward instead of backward to get out. She pushed out all the boards of the wall in front of her, but it did not hurt the car. She backed out all right, and Dad nailed the boards back. Dad built the stall and box and had the haymow filled when he decided to keep a saddle horse there.

We went in the barn and up the ladder. There was lots of hay. A farmer had just filled the mow for Dad a few days ago. I walked on the springy hay and found a good place to burrow in. I spread the hay apart with my hands and arms and crawled on my hands and knees into the hay. It was dry and sticky and it smelled pretty good. We got scratched and full of hay leaves and stems. The others followed as I made a tunnel across the loft, then they branched out and made their own tunnels. I came out over by the hole where we pitch hay down for Cactus. When I looked out over the hay I saw it move where they were working through. I yelled, "Let's meet in the middle." They started working toward the center of the hay and I did, too. Pretty soon we bumped into each other and then we stood up and worked our way to the top. We were hot, dusty, sweaty, scratched up and our hair was full of hay. We decided to tunnel back to the ladder and go to the pump.

There Baldy pumped the handle and Virgene and I ran the water over our hands, arms and faces, and took drinks. Then I pumped while Baldy washed off and drank out of the blue granite cup. The water was so cold. It tasted and felt good. Even Pal came over and lapped up what he could. The cat didn't bother.

Baldy was looking around. He said, "Let's go behind the ferns and crawl under the porch." He led off and we followed. Mother has nice big ferns along the north side of the house. Our front porch, on the east side, is high enough so we can easily crawl under it, but we bump our heads if we try to sit up. It was cool and sort of damp behind the ferns and had that kind of earthy smell that comes from wet ground and plants and old leaves. We took lots of time to enjoy the coolness and looked out through the lacy ferns. We could see across our yard, between two big apple trees and into the pasture just north of us. There were a couple of cows in the pasture, good old black and white Holsteins. They belong to Mr. Skene who lives in the next house north of us. The cows were not doing anything except eating grass. There is plenty of that.

Finally we crawled under the porch. It is a big porch going all across the front of the house. There are bushes around it so it is all dark underneath. As our eyes got used to the light we found old boards and bricks and a soggy ball, but nothing any good. It smelled like dirt and old lumber and was a little damp. We crawled all around, even under the steps, and sat scrunched up just enjoying the shade.

When we got tired of that we crawled out into the sunshine on the south side of the house. There our lot is right next to old Mr. Harbach's garden. His lot is so close to ours that the coal wagon can't deliver coal to our coal bin through the basement window without putting one set of wheels on his land. That upsets him and he comes and complains about it. That is in the fall when he does not have anything in the garden. Dad just told him he was sorry, but we had to have coal and if he could show where there was any damage he would try to make it right. Nothing was hurt. Old Mr. Harbach just likes to grumble. Dad can take care of it all right but when Mr. Harbach yells at us kids he sort of scares us.

Toward the back of our house, on the south side, there is another place almost like a tunnel made by big lilac, elderberry and currant bushes on one side, and the house and screened-in porch on the other. That is a cool shady place. We went there and picked a few currants and then sat down in the shade. There were ground cherries in their thin, tissue covers like little magic lanterns near the ground. We like to eat ground cherries raw, but Mother makes great pies out of them.

When we were tired of sitting there we went out in the light again and started toward the garden. I thought we might find some ripe tomatoes. They are good to eat right off the plant. Mother saw me and called out, "Oh Bill, I didn't know where you were. Would you and your friends like some cookies and milk?"

We sure would. So we ran to the pump and washed up fast, then to the kitchen table in the screened porch. Ma gave us big sugar cookies and glasses of cold milk. She said, "You look like real hayseeds. Were you up in the haymow?"

I said, "Yes," and she said, "Well, be careful."

After our cookies and milk we went out to the back part of the chicken yard, where it is like a woods. There was one more thing to go through. It was a nice big barrel on its side. It used to be a rain barrel but it came apart. The bottom rotted out. It won't hold rainwater, but it is just right to crawl through. We went through it several times.

The shadows were longer so we thought it might be getting toward supper time. Baldy said, "Well, so long. See you tomorrow." Virgene said, "Yeah, so long, see you tomorrow." I said, "So long," and we all headed home.

BIG DAY

Tonight I think I am all frazzled out. That is what Mother says when she is very tired and it sounds like the way I feel. It is only Thursday, September 27, 1923, but today was Lena's Big Day. School was out and everybody was downtown to have a good time. They did it last year and liked it so well they decided to do it again.

Streets were blocked off in the main part of town so we did not have to worry about cars or wagons. I don't think I ever saw so many people here. Over a thousand people live in Lena. Last month at Camp Meeting, they said there were four thousand who came here from everywhere. I know there were more than seven hundred cars parked on the street and in the part of the Camp Ground where we usually play baseball and volleyball. I thought there were more in town today. All my friends and I had fun downtown and east of town, where the balloon went up.

It took a lot of work to get ready for a big day like this. Many men and women thought up the things to do and organized it to bring everything together and to spread the word around so people in other

towns and on farms would know. The Lena Volunteer
Firemen did the most. They were already organized
and used to working together. We have two big fire
trucks in the fire station, which is in the same building
as the town hall. The library is upstairs. If anyone
has a fire, they call the telephone operator and she
turns on the fire siren. The firemen hear it and,
wherever they are, rush to the fire station, put on
their coats and helmets, find out where the fire is,
and jump on the trucks. They go as fast as they can
to whatever is burning and try to put it out. They
are very quick and they know what to do because
they practice.

In town we have a tall water tower built out of
stone and brick. The water from our town well is
pumped up there and then it flows through pipes all
over to the fire hydrants and also to people's houses
who have city water. We have a pump in our yard,
but many houses have city water now.

The water tower is very tall and we are all proud
of it. It was built almost thirty years ago. Mr. Eells
said a funny thing happened when they built it in
the early winter and had the stone work nearly up.
On Christmas Day, neighbors heard a noise and when
they looked at the water tower they saw it had fallen
down. It just collapsed because there was too much
water in the mortar, Mr. Eells said. Everybody was
mad. They did not think it was very funny. They gave
the job to a different company and then it was built
right. It surely is solid now.

Then they put in pipes and water hydrants for
the fire hoses and everybody felt safer. Before that,
all the water firemen could use to fight a fire was

whatever they could carry in the tank truck and however much the house had in its cistern. Some homes had large individual water reservoirs underground, and in two or three places around town they had big underground reservoirs to store water for fires. But none of that helped as much as the fire hydrants.

Fires are just terrible. Sometimes a barn will catch fire all by itself. They call it spontaneous combustion from hay that was put in the mow before it was dry enough. It is lucky if they can get any animals out of the barn and maybe save other buildings nearby. They can hardly ever put out a barn fire. Last winter at the Wernike farm north of town there was an awful fire. They had an acetylene system for lights and it blew up. The whole house blew apart. The mother and little boy were killed and everybody else was burned and hurt. My dad went on the emergency call and brought the little girl to town. Then he and her grandmother took her to the St. Francis hospital in Freeport. The fire department went to the farm, but all they could do was save other buildings. That helps some, anyway.

There have been terrible fires in Lena because most of the buildings are wooden and there are flames in fire places, stoves, furnaces, candles and lamps. Now, with electric light and better furnaces and a water system, things are not so bad as they used to be.

Firemen have had experience working together and they like to do good things. It was natural for them to help put on the Big Day for our town. I could not believe all there was to do. I had a list of concession stands from the Lena Star and we tried to go to everything, but there were even more than they had listed. There were stands that sold cotton candy and popcorn and there were stands where we could buy chances on things, like dolls or toys or blankets. They would spin a big wheel to see who won.

At another stand a man had little turtles that he would put in the middle of a big circle on a flat piece of tin. The turtles were numbered. He held a lighted candle under the middle of the tin so the turtles would hurry away from the hot spot. The first turtle to cross the outside circle won, and whoever had that number got the prize.

At other places we could buy chances to throw baseballs at pieces of wood shaped like milk bottles to win prizes. There was a rifle target range with moving iron ducks and regular targets. My friends and I were pretty good at that, but we did not have enough money to shoot very much. The men used the concession stands and the bingo game the most. We watched.

They had a tall pole with a bell at the top. A strong man could swing the sledge hammer and drive a piece of metal to the top to ring the bell. Then he got a prize. Usually it did not go that high and the concession man just kept the money the man gave him to try.

There was a merry-go-round that we all rode. It was fun. But the most fun were the contests. There was a girls' cracker eating contest. The one who could eat the crackers and swallow them first won. They

did not use any water to help. Helen Loomis won.
I didn't know how she could get them to go down
so fast.

They had a women's sawing contest. The women
sawed through a big oak plank to see who could do
it first. Landis Hutmacher won the fat man's race
and Elizabeth Doll won the girls' foot race. She was
really speedy.

My friend Vernon Inman—we call him Andy
because he is tall like Andy Gump in the cartoon—
won the melon eating contest and he did all right
in the flour contest. He was second in that one. They
rigged up a trough and put silver dollars and lots
of nickles in it and then covered them over with flour
real deep. The boys in the contest had to blow away
the flour and pick up coins with their teeth. They
could not use their hands. They just had one minute
to see how much they could get. All of us who tried
got to keep whatever we picked out. That was good,
but what a mess!

In the pie eating contest, Alfred Rampenthal ate
the most the fastest. There was a nail-driving contest
for women. They hammered and banged away and
everybody laughed and yelled to encourage them.

Andy was second in the bicycle race. It was right
down Main Street. One of the best races was the mule
race. That was on Main Street, too. The mules ran,
then got excited by all the noisy people and stopped.
They were balky mules, the men said. Finally, Leslie
Uhe got his to go enough to cross the finish line.
He won and pretty soon Noel Wachlin persuaded his
to go ahead and win second place.

We did not have any track for an auto race, so they had a slow Ford race. The winner was a Mr. Haubach who took the longest time to go a block of Main Street without killing his motor. There was a sack race for men. They hopped along with their feet in a sack. Alfred Rampenthal won that, too. Then they had a three-legged race for men with the legs next to each other tied together so they had to cooperate really well to go fast.

Somebody set up a pole, put some money on top of it, then greased it. That was another mess, but a man did get up and grab the money before he slid back down.

They had a couple of team games. In the tug of war contest, the men from the south side of town pulled the north-side team over the line. I was not very happy about that, because I live on the north side, but we lived on the south side when we first came to town. On the school grounds, the Lena High School baseball team played the Pearl City High School team and won twenty-three to four.

At noon, before all this started, there were free roast beef sandwiches for everyone and coffee for the grown-ups. About five o'clock we all went to the east edge of town where a man from Chicago was putting hot air from a little fire on the ground into a big balloon. His name is Ben Grew and he had done this lots of times, but it looked scary to us. The balloon slowly filled with hot air and when it was full it tried to go up but several men held it with ropes. Mr. Grew had a parachute on his back and he got ready by sitting on a trapeze and holding its ropes. The men let go of the balloon and up it went. Mr. Grew waved and we waved. When he was up high, he jumped off the trapeze and then his parachute opened like a big umbrella. He floated down just as nice as you please. The balloon came down by itself. It did not drift too far. He went in a truck to get it. We thought it was exciting.

This evening there is a big free dance in the street with music by the Lena Imperial Band. They have been playing off and on all afternoon. Mr. Nuss is the director and the band sounds good. They have practiced together a long time. My friends and I don't dance, but we go and watch. The high school kids and the grown-ups really like to dance. Some people do not think boys and girls should dance together, others think it is all right. It looks all right to me, if they want to.

My friends and I split up and went home after listening to the band a while. I had a hamburger sandwich and a glass of Coca Cola at the Opera House Cafe for supper. When I got home, I had a big glass of milk and now I am going to turn in. Frazzled!

BILLY

Man! Am I full! We just had Thanksgiving dinner a little while ago and everything tasted good. Mother said she didn't see how anyone my size could hold so much. She said she was happy I liked it and I sure did. There was a big roasted turkey full of dressing. It was in the middle of the dining room table before Dad carved it into slices for us. There were sweet potatoes in their own skins and regular potatoes all mashed up and gravy and corn and beets and cranberries and mince pie and ice cream and lots of other stuff like salad and relishes. I didn't think I would ever get full, but I did. My two sisters are not very big. Mother and Dad are bigger, but they did not eat as much as I did. Mother was probably right about me being her champion eater.

Now all I can do is just sit here on the davenport and sort of think and remember. It is windy and cold out doors and I do not feel like going out right now anyway. The leaves are all gone and it is gray and cloudy. I am thinking how glad I am that I had my billy goat. Thankful, I guess, because it is Thanksgiving Day.

DAD CALLS ME JACK

Last spring Dad brought home a frisky little goat which a farmer friend had given him. They called him a kid just like they do me. He was quick and jumpy and had long legs with little hooves and a hard little head but he was cuddly and friendly, too. He couldn't eat grass and other stuff yet, but had to have milk from a bottle. Dad took an empty ketchup bottle and filled it with milk and then tied a finger he had cut off a rubber glove onto it. He cut a little hole in the end of the finger to make it like a nipple and then put it into Billy's mouth. He was hungry and he sucked on it right away. He pulled so hard he got more milk out than he could swallow and got it all over his face and me, too. We fed him his bottle several times a day. Sometimes he was really impatient and he would bite and pull the nipple and get milk all over. But he kept growing and pretty soon he could eat grass and almost everything else. He liked labels off tin cans and even chewed on the cans. We tried to keep him tied on a long rope or in our little barn with Cactus, my dad's horse.

I let him run loose so I could play with him and sometimes he got away by himself and that made problems. When he was little he did not have any horns, but soon I could feel little bumps growing on his head and by the end of summer he had big horns. Of course by then he was pretty big, too. In the spring, when he was little, everybody played with him. Even my sister Virginia, who is five years old, did. She would pet him and pull her hand back quick when he tried to suck her fingers and she would run with him. Margery was too little to play with him. She is only two. But she liked to watch him and pet him when I held him still.

He grew fast and it was not long until he was too rough for the girls. Virginia liked to swing on a tree swing Dad put up on our big old Russet apple tree. She would swing herself back and forth in the swing. Billy liked to butt things and people with his head. He would watch Virginia swinging back and forth and then he would run at her from behind and just as she swung down from the forward part of her swing he would butt her from behind and push her out of the swing. He thought it was fun and it sure looked funny, but she did not like it very much. I had to make him stop.

Toward the end of summer he was big enough so I could ride him. Sometimes he would run across the yard at me, like he was going to butt me with his horns. Just as he got to me I would grab hold of his horns and jump on his back and we would go for a ride till he got tired or we both fell down. It was a lot of fun. Some of my friends tried it, but it did not work as well for them. Baldy got pretty good at it. I had more practice. Bob was the one who never could quite get along with Billy.

One afternoon, Billy was loose and he took after Bob. Bob got scared, I guess, and started to run up the hill. Billy chased him past old man Harbach's place and I was running after them laughing so hard I couldn't run very fast. Bob ran across the street and up on Mammoser's porch. They have a big white house and a railing around their porch. We don't have a railing around our porch. Bob went as far as he could go and Billy ran right up to him and held him against the wall with his head and those hard old horns. When I got there I grabbed Billy's collar and pulled him away. I was laughing so hard I could hardly do it. Bob was really mad and had his feelings hurt and me laughing didn't help much. My goat liked to play and have fun and I knew what he was thinking about. He didn't mean to hurt anyone, but he grew and his horns grew and pretty soon he hurt people without realizing it.

Baldy and Woody and I tried to hitch him to Baldy's coaster wagon. We did not have a regular wagon for goats or ponies but we rigged up a rope harness and tied him to Baldy's wagon. We had a good rough ride all right, but we found out we could not make him go where we wanted to go. He just went where he wanted to go and if he wanted to chase something we had a fast ride.

When fall came and I had to go back to school, it was harder to take care of Billy. We did not have a fenced in place for him. He got out of Dad's chicken yard and the barn and even chewed off his rope. Nobody but me could handle him. So Dad talked to me about it and told me maybe we should give him to an old man who lived at the edge of town and needed a goat. I really hated to give up Billy, but I could see we could not take care of him anymore, so I said it would be all right.

I hope Billy has a good home there. I never saw him again.

CHRISTMAS

It feels good to be in my feather bed. I sink down and the mattress comes up beside me and a soft comforter goes over and then there is a blanket and a quilt on top of that. Ma calls it a crazy quilt because it has patches of all different colors. They are sewed together with little tiny stitches and it is fun to trace over them with my finger. I don't think it is really crazy because they all come out even at the edges. My pillow is soft, too. I can wad it up any way I want so it feels just right. There was snow on my covers this morning where it blew in through the window. Ma says I have to have fresh air, but sometimes it is really cold. I stay warm in bed because it comes up around me and I have warm pajamas on. Some of my pajamas have feet in them and some do not. Sometimes I wear socks to bed. The reason I was thinking about all this is that I am still in bed, because I have a cold and Ma said it would be good for me to stay in for a while. Last night I was coughing quite a bit and I did not feel very good.

She gave me warm lemonade and warm tea to drink and then she put a mustard plaster on my chest. My dad is a doctor and he said it was all right. Anyway, I feel better this morning and I do not have to cough all the time. It is sort of nice to stay in bed and I can write in my theme book.

You see, yesterday was Christmas and the day before was Christmas Eve and I guess that is how I got a cold. My sister Virginia is five and my sister Margery is two and they have been really excited about Christmas. Several days ago we had the Sunday School Christmas Pageant. Some of the other guys and I were all dressed up in our bathrobes with towels around our heads for turbans. A couple had cardboard crowns. I was a Wise Man but I didn't have a crown, only a turban. We wore robes like they did in the East, but theirs were all rich and royal and ours were just bathrobes. They brought the little baby Jesus very great presents, but we pretended. I guess his parents looked after the gifts for him because he was so little. Virginia was an angel and she was fixed up real pretty. Margery sat on Mother's lap and watched. She seemed to like it all right, at least she did not cry.

The day after that Dad brought home our Christmas tree. It is as tall as he is and all green and full. A farmer friend told him where it was on his farm and Dad chopped it down. He put it in the trunk of his car to haul it home. I helped him bring it into the kitchen, and there he nailed cross boards up a little way to brace it. Then it stood up by itself in the living room. Ma covered the base with cotton to make it look like snow.

She had some tinsel that we put on the tree, and some artificial snow, but the best was what we made ourselves. Ma popped some popcorn and we ate some but most of it we strung on thread using one of her needles. When we had a long string of it, we draped it on the tree branches so it was pretty. Then we made other strings out of cranberries and put them around the tree, too. Dad placed the star on the top of the tree. It made the top bend over so he had to put some wire on to hold it up straight. The last thing was putting the candles on. Dad and I did that. The candle holders clamped to the tree branches. We placed them very carefully so the candle flame would not catch the tree on fire. Dad explained about that and when the candles were lit he always stayed close by. But we only lit them Christmas Eve and it wasn't time yet. I thought the tree was beautiful. There were lots of other things on it, like glass balls, little angels and Santa Clauses. I think Mother put cut- out parts of Christmas cards on, also.

My sisters and I would look at the tree from time to time. Packages just appeared around it, one now and one after a while, and they had names on them, but Mother said not to touch them until Christmas Eve. I knew that would only be a couple of days, but Virginia kept asking if it was Christmas Eve yet. Margery would have gotten into them without asking, but Mother kept her away. They were both excited about Santa Claus, and Mother told them over and over that we would have our own Christmas presents on Christmas Eve and then, while they were asleep, Santa would come and leave presents for them and we would find them on Christmas morning.

Mother planned to have a big dinner on Christmas Day.

That is pretty much the way it was. On Christmas Eve we were all happy and excited and talked a lot. After supper, Dad had us sit around the Christmas tree. Mother played some Christmas songs on the piano and she and Dad sang. My sisters and I tried to sing, too. We probably were not very good, but we liked it and tried hard. Dad said a prayer about little baby Jesus and how He came down from Heaven to help all of us, even though He didn't have to. It made me feel sad that He went to so much trouble, but I was glad that He lived, and I hoped He had fun when He was a boy over there in the Holy Land.

Then we could open our presents. The girls got dolls and clothes. I got a coaster wagon that I really like, but I'll have to wait till next spring to use it. Then I got some lace-up high boots that I can use right now. The snow is deep and it is so cold. There was a shirt and some handkerchiefs, too, but the wagon and boots were what I thought about the most.

We did not forget my dog, Pal, either. He had some extra good bones and he chewed on them and grinned like dogs do.

Pretty soon it was time to go to bed. So we put out cookies and milk for Santa. Dad said he would leave the front door open a little for Santa to use because we do not have a fireplace. Dad said Santa would not want to slide down the chimney into a furnace.

Yesterday morning the girls got up early and they squealed and yelled when they found the cookies and milk gone and some more dolls and things to play with, and they were really tickled. I was happy with a new knife and some mittens I could use to go with my new boots.

So just as soon as I could I put on all my winter clothes and my new boots and a cap with ear flaps and my new mittens, and Pal and I went outdoors.

I had a wonderful time tromping down the snow and making paths and making snowballs to throw at the trees. It was cold and I came back in the house after a while. My mittens and boots were kind of wet. When I warmed up, my fingers tingled and hurt and so did my toes and my cheeks. Ma said it was frostbite and I shouldn't stay out so long. In a little while it stopped hurting. I put my mittens and boots over a register to dry and warm up. I stood over another one to do the same.

Everything smelled so good. Mother had a big roasted goose in the middle of the table and lots of other things around. Dad got the goose from a farmer and fixed it so Mother could cook it, and she made two kinds of potatoes, bread, jam, lettuce and apple sauce, corn, and mince pie. After that I felt good so I went back outdoors. Two of my friends came and we built a snowman and a fort and threw lots of snowballs. When they went home and I came back in the house, I had frostbite again. It took a long time for my hands and feet to quit hurting and Mother said she was afraid I would catch a bad cold.

That was when she made the hot lemonade and had me get into my warm flannel pajamas. Later she gave me some hot tea and some soup. She made a mustard plaster and put it on my chest. I didn't like the smell very much but it sure felt warm. She gave me some honey mixed with vinegar for my cough. That was not too bad. Anyway, I slept almost all night and now I feel better. I hope you had a wonderful, happy Christmas, too.

ICE AND SNOW

It seems like something always happens. Now I have this scrape and pain low on my right side and Dad says it's a wonder I don't have a rupture. All I did was ski downhill back of the Camp Grounds.

Earlier this afternoon a bunch of us kids went out to the pond for a hockey game. For once the ice was smooth enough for good skating. We swept off the snow and marked goals. We put on our skates, some clamp-on and some regular shoe skates. I have new shoe skates that I am not used to, but I like to wear them. It has been a bright winter day, below freezing but hardly any wind, and a great day to be outdoors.

I guess we are supposed to have four players on each side in hockey, but we go ahead with whoever wants to play. Usually we have from three to five on each side. We use my puck and everybody has his own stick, some bought and some home-made. We have lots of fun, do a lot of skating, get in some good whacks that regular hockey players would not do, and play till we are tired. Players come and go. We try to keep score, but sometimes we forget and nobody cares too much. We do play hard, even if sometimes it slips our minds which team we are on or which goal is ours. When we are older, if we play on regular teams, we will have to be more careful about those things.

I played hockey about an hour or so. Then I was tired and my ankles were so weak and played-out that I decided to come home. I could not stay there and rest because we did not have any warm place. Inside I was sweated up, but outside my hands and feet and face were cold. My puck was still in use; if I took it, they could use a mashed-down tin can, but I didn't see one. Baldy wanted to play some more. He said he would take care of the puck, so I walked home carrying my skates and my nice new stick Dad bought at Messing's Store in Freeport. It is banged up a little and I have taped it to make it stronger, but it is just fine.

When we get all excited about putting the puck in the goal, sometimes we swing the sticks around pretty hard and higher than we are supposed to. Somebody is always getting hit. Today I have some bumps on my head and chest and back, but they hardly hurt at all because my heavy winter clothes and knitted stocking cap protected me. It is a good half-mile home. I took it easy and my feet and ankles gradually felt better. At home I thawed out my fingers and nose. A little while indoors was enough. It was too beautiful a day to stay inside. The snow just sparkled in the sunshine. Behind and below the tops of drifts were sharp black shadows. Everything is so different from the green of summer.

Yesterday was a good day, too, but more cloudy. Several of us went to Nudd's hill near the school to slide our sleds. Woody, Baldy, Virginia, Ellen and Aaron were there when I was. There were not too many cars. We rode our sleds down the hill right on the street where it was hard-packed and slippery. Sometimes they close the street for a couple of blocks so kids can use it. People don't like to drive on it when it is so slick anyway. We had a great time belly-flopping on our Flexible Flyers and racing down as fast as we could go. Now and then we would go two at a time, one on top of the other. You have to be careful about that because it is possible to bend the runner-bracings of the sled that way.

It is neat to have two good winter days in a row. Mother said I shouldn't overdo it, but she understood that I wanted to try out my skis on the good snow. My skis are only about three-quarter size, but they fit me. I have not used them very much. Pictures of skiers show them using a pole in each hand going across the country. My one pole is made out of a broomstick, but it helps.

I carried my skis and pole to the big field west of the Camp Ground. Over the fence, I put on the skis and slid them cross- country down the first slope, then across the frozen creek and up the western hill. After a couple of trips back and forth to the north end of the field, I thought it would be fun to go as fast as I could downhill and maybe jump the creek. There was a place where the west bank was higher than the other. I thought I could do it.

At the top of the hill on the west, I started down going east, toward the Camp Ground. Using my pole, I went as fast as I could. I was going lickety-split when I got to the creek. Evidently I was not going fast enough because I tipped in the air and lost my balance. I came down hard on the east bank of the creek and lit on my ski pole. I must have stuck it out in front of me on the right. The point of the pole hit the snow and ground first and I came down on top of it. My abdomen hit it near my right groin and I thought it was going through me. It tore all the buttons off my pants. My side hurt so much I could hardly get up out of the snow. I was clear down on the dirt underneath. In a little while I got on my feet, but I did not feel like skiing anymore. I just needed to go home. The walk home was a lot longer than walking out.

Mother had me lie down on the davenport, then she called Dad. I am afraid he will get tired of coming to see what is the matter with me. He said, "It is a wonder you do not have a rupture or worse." He thought I would be all right if I would stay quiet. So I am being very quiet, but if it is a good day again tomorrow, maybe I can try the skis just on the level.

ROLLER SKATING

You wouldn't believe what a nice day this was. It is Valentine's Day. We have had lots of cold snowy weather, but the last few days have been warm; today was sunny, and the sidewalks are clean and dry all over town. There are patches of dirty snow, but not on the sidewalk. That means all of us kids got out our roller skates that we haven't been able to use all winter and went skating.

This morning I called Woody and Baldy and we decided to meet at the Opera House Cafe downtown. We like to go there anyway for ice cream and stuff and usually we find other kids either there or somewhere downtown. I put on regular shoes and fitted my skates on them and tightened the clamps with my skate key until they really bit into the edges of the leather soles. I do not like for them to come loose and I don't like to stop and fix them every little while either.

I skated right up the hill to the railroad depot, crossed the tracks, then went to the left down Main Street. You always have to be careful skating on Main Street because there are grown-up people there that you don't want to bump. The restaurant is run by Mr. and Mrs. Benninger. They are real nice and they have a little boy we call "Shay" because of the way he says his "S's." He is cheerful and big for his age, but he is too young to play with us. There were a few other kids there, boys and girls. They were having ice cream cones and sundaes and things. Woody got a chocolate soda, Baldy got a butterscotch sundae, and I had an Eskimo Pie. I think they taste so good, with thin chocolate coating over a vanilla ice cream bar. I don't know if Eskimos made them or if someone just thought they were something Eskimos ought to like, but they are one of my favorite things to eat.

Pretty soon we all went out and skated toward the school and down Nudd's hill. We met Virginia. She was skating, too, and decided to go along with us. I was glad to see her. She is tall, has brown hair, and I think she is the prettiest girl in our class. Her father is a partner with Mr. John Diestelmeier in the Rech and Diestelmeier Clothing Store. I think maybe he runs the Lena Casket Company, too. She is very smart in school and when she looks at a person it is real nice and friendly. She is interested in things like roller skating and tennis that many of us played last summer.

We sort of strung out and skated down the big hill. Sometimes there are cracks in the sidewalk to watch out for and some of the sidewalk is old and rough. We took turns leading. We went fast or slow depending on the kind of sidewalk or whether it was uphill. All of us had skated all over town before. We knew just what to expect and where to be extra careful.

It was really fun to skate and feel the breezes and feel free. It had been so long since we had done it.

We skated past the Poultry House on Oak Street, beside where we used to live. There is a place right where the sidewalk turns to go on Oak Street that the root of a big old maple tree has pushed up the sidewalk and tilted it a little. Somebody nearly always takes a spill on that and someone did today, but I don't remember who it was.

Sometimes we swung each other along. That is when one skater takes another one's hand and skates fast and pulls him on ahead real fast, but coasting. Then that person turns and does the same thing for the first one. Woody skated with Virginia often, but once in a while Baldy and I got a chance to skate with her, too. We always tried to swing her extra good so she could coast a long way.

As we skated, some of the boys and girls would leave to go home and others would join in with us. It seemed like everyone was out. When we finally went across the railroad tracks at the Kennedy and Ellis garage to skate on the north side of town, we went west on the street next to the tracks that they call Railroad Street, and pretty soon we were near the depot at the top of our hill. Old man Harter was in his shoe store. He had moved a cobbler's bench to the doorway because it was such a nice day. He waved a hammer at us as we skated by. We stopped at Dr. Salter's house near the depot to catch our breath and rest a little.

Then we started down the hill. We skated as fast as we could go. There were not any cars coming on Lena Street so we didn't have to wait, but of course we had to walk across the rough street before going down the best part of the hill toward our house. We stopped in our yard to rest a little before going on to the Camp Ground.

When we pulled in at our place, I saw my bicycle leaning against the back porch and I had an idea. I asked Virginia if she would like to go down the hill skating, me pulling her with my bike. She thought that would be fun. So when the others started on toward the Camp Ground, I took my skates off, found a piece of rope to tie to the bike saddle post, and we went back up to Lena Street.

She held on to the rope and I swung on my bike and started. Pulling her downhill was easy. We were going faster than she had ever skated before and she liked it. She is a really good skater. The trouble was that at the far edge of our lot there is about a two-inch ridge in the sidewalk where a new stretch of walk begins. We are used to it and just jump our bikes over it without thinking, or jump over it with our skates. But she wasn't used to it because she lives on the south side of town.

Well, I jumped my bike over all right, but her skates caught on the ridge and she fell down full-length on the hard sidewalk. I skidded to a stop and ran back to help her get up. I felt awful. I knew it was my fault. I helped her sit up and she had scrapes on her hands and a bump on her chin. She said it was not too bad. I thought it was. She was a good sport and did not even cry. She said she wanted to go on. I put my skates on again and we skated to the Camp Ground where the kids had stopped.

Most of them had not missed us, but Woody wondered where we had been. I told him what had happened and she showed him her hands and chin. All he said was, "Gee whiz," but I could tell he felt sorry for her.

It was too muddy and soft to play in the Camp Ground, so we skated back toward town. When we got near the railroad tracks we decided we were tired and had skated enough for one day. We split up. When I said good-bye to Virginia I told her again how sorry I was that she was hurt. I was afraid she would not want to be friends anymore, but she said, "That's all right; it doesn't hurt much now."

DAD'S BIRTHDAY

Today is my dad's birthday. It is March 4, and a cold, windy day. Part of the time it was snowing, too, just like a blizzard. Dad worked in his office all day, seeing sick people. I suppose he made some calls to see sick people in their houses, too. But this evening he was home for dinner and Mother had made it extra special for him.

I could hardly eat, I was so excited about the present I had for him. Dad likes to hunt. In the hunting season he goes out early in the morning with some friend, usually a farmer who knows where the ducks and squirrels and rabbits and snipe and prairie chickens are. One of his friends told me Dad is a good shot but that he doesn't always bring the game home. Sometimes he gives it to them.

Maybe part of the reason is that Mother does not really like to cook game animals very much, even when Dad gets them all ready. Anyway, he likes to get outdoors and hunt. He says it reminds him of the old days when he was growing up on the farm. He has just one single-shot 12-gauge shotgun. It has a big kick and sometimes bruises his shoulder. He said one time he was shooting at a bird in the sky and the gun drove his heels in the ground.

So when I was thinking about what he would like and looking at the stores downtown, I found something at Pappy Wingart's. That is a wonderful store. He calls it "The Store of Most Anything" and that must be right. It is like looking at everything in a Montgomery Ward catalog all spread out and bunched up in front of you. The store is not really very big, but it has lots of shelves, counters, boxes, barrels and corners. When you go in, there is a door to the right which opens into a little room separate from the rest of the store. That is where Mr. Wingart makes cigars. It smells good, but I wouldn't want to smoke one of those cigars. He has many blocks of wood with cigar-shaped places in them. Sometimes we watch while he takes some long pieces of tobacco leaf, shapes them like a cigar, wraps a special wrapper leaf around it, licks it with his tongue to make it stay in place, and then fits it into one of the cigar shaped holes. That makes certain they are all the same size and helps them hold their shape better. He puts another pattern block on top to be sure the cigars are the same all around and then he sets them to one side for a while. When he takes them out they are his own special hand-made cigars and he sells them.

They must grow tobacco around here some place but I haven't seen any growing. I saw some long brown leaves drying in the tobacco barn on High Point, though.

Mr. Wingart has so many things in his store it is hard to get around. People call him Pappy and I guess he doesn't mind, but Mother does not think that is polite. There are buggy whips, lots of gloves, corn-husking pegs, soapstone foot-warmers, mouse traps, traps for rabbits, muskrat, mink and foxes, percolator tops, rubber boots, paper fans, and too many other things to count. But what I had been watching all fall and winter and saving up my allowance and chore money for hung on the wall.

It was a Stevens single-shot .22-caliber rifle and it cost seven dollars and fifty cents. About a week before Dad's birthday I had enough money. I took it up to Mr. Wingart and told him I wanted to buy the gun as a birthday present for my dad. I don't think he was surprised, because I had looked at it so many times. He took it off the wall and said, "I think that will be a nice present. And here is something for you, too." He handed me a long strip of whang leather rawhide lacing. It is real neat. I can use it to lace my boots or to tie up stuff.

I carried the rifle home just as proud as could be. I kept it up out of the snow. I met Mr. Eells (everybody calls him Cash) and he asked me what I was hunting. He and Dad are good friends. I told him it was a present for my dad and he asked to see it. He looked at it very carefully and then said, "That is a good sturdy piece and it will be accurate. I'll bet Doc gets a lot of rabbits with that."

Mr. Eells knows all about guns because he was in the army, even before the Great War. He was in the cavalry and helped chase Pancho Villa down into Mexico. Then he trained other soldiers to shoot during the war. Maybe sometime he will teach me all about it.

When I got home, Mother helped me wrap my present. It looked fancy and pretty, but you could still just about tell what it was.

When Dad came home, Mother hugged and kissed him at the door and said, "Happy Birthday, Otis!"

He said, "Thanks, Honey," and seemed real happy. He looked at the packages on the buffet. Mother had her present and Virginia's and Margery's presents all wrapped up and lying there with mine.

She saw him look at them and said, "Now, supper is ready. You wash up and come to the table. You can open your gifts later."

For supper we had fried chicken and corn bread with butter and jelly and mashed potatoes and other things that Dad likes. It tasted good, but for once I did not eat much. I was thinking about the rifle and hoping he would like it. At the end, Mother brought out an angel food cake with white icing and lots of candles, all lit up and burning.

Dad said, "My, I didn't think it would look like so many. That's enough to warm up the whole room. That is sure a beautiful cake, Hon."

She said, "Well, you're not forty yet, so it's not too bad." Dad made a wish and blew out the candles. We all made happy wishes for him. We said ours out loud, but he did not say what his wish was. They said that was the way to make it come true.

After we ate our pieces of cake, my sisters and I started for the presents, but Mother thought it would be better one at a time. She gave a package to Virginia to take to him. It was a fine white shirt from Mother. Dad opened Margery's package and found some pairs of socks which he liked and said he needed very much. Then Virginia took hers over and it was a good pair of gloves. He liked those, too.

Then it was my turn. I picked up my present very carefully and gave it to him. He lifted it, turned and handled it before opening the package. "Is this what I think it is?" he asked.

"I don't know; what do you think?" I asked back.

He opened it quickly and looked it over, then put it to his shoulder and sighted along the barrel.

"Jack," he said, "this is just great. Thank you. We will have a lot of fun with this."

I was so happy I almost cried. Now I am hungry. Maybe I can get something out of the ice box.

ORDERING STUFF

This is a chilly rainy day. It is springtime, but there is no sunshine at all. It is a gloomy Saturday. I do not have to be in school, but it is better indoors than outside today. When I look out I can see everything wet and dripping and little streams of water running down the window panes. Mother says it is a good day to catch up on work and be sure to wipe my shoes when I come in.

She let me help polish the silverware. Maybe that is work, but it is nice to see it shine. Mother has some good knives and forks and spoons that she and Dad saved up to get. She said that it is good to use it all the time because then we can enjoy it and it looks even better with patina. I didn't know what that meant. So she said, "When these pieces are used they get lots of tiny little marks on them. That is patina and it shows loving use."

For a long time after the silver was polished I looked at catalogs. There are so many pictures to see and things I could order if I had the money. The Sears, Roebuck and Company and Montgomery Ward and Company catalogs are the biggest. They have just about everything anyone could want. Mother says we can get most anything downtown, but sometimes she orders something. Whenever we get new big catalogs we take the old ones to the outhouse and use them to clean up with. Even there it is kind of fun to sit and look at the pictures until you need to use the paper. Uncle Clem and Uncle Otto put buckets of fresh corn cobs in their outhouses, but they have catalogs, too.

I think the catalogs I like best are from Francis Bannerman and Son of New York City and the International Trading Company of Brooklyn. These are mine. I wrote to them from advertisements in Boy's Life magazine. I wrote to Johnson, Smith and Company, too. They have all kinds of funny things for jokes and toys and badges. I already got a Big Bang cannon from them. It makes a big noise when I put some water in it, then some of their special powder, and press on the button at the back end of the cannon. That makes a spark and off it goes.

The Bannerman catalog is more serious. Mr. Bannerman bought most of the guns and saddles and swords and canteens and supplies left over after the Civil War and other things the army and navy were through with since then. Many of them are from the Great War. There are a few real old men here in town who are "old soldiers." They fought in the Civil War. There are a few from the Spanish-American War and lots of soldiers from the Great War.

That was just a few years ago. Now on Decoration Day the soldiers put on their uniforms and march in the parade. Ben Dameier works at Kennedy and Ellis Garage. He was a sergeant. Zeke Altenbern, maybe his name is Harry, always marches with them. He never says much, but one of his medals is a distinguished service cross and Dad says that means he was an extra brave soldier. Cash Eells is the one I know best. He was in the cavalry and went down into Mexico, but he did not go over to Europe. He was such a good shot he had to stay here to teach new soldiers how to shoot. The Goebel brothers are Joe and John. They live on a farm north of town and sometimes Dad hires one of them to take him on a bobsled to make calls in the winter time. Albert Diestelmeier is a farmer, too. He likes to talk about the army and his eyes crinkle up when he smiles. He likes to play the fiddle. They say 'Friday' Ritzman was a tough soldier, but he smiles and laughs now. Mr. Gale, the grocer, was in the army, too. There are others I don't know who march in the parade. The "old soldiers" can't march that far. They ride in cars.

When I look at all the army and navy things in the Bannerman catalog I think about the soldiers and sailors and what all they have to do in war. I do not have very much money, but I save up some so that I can buy something. Today I just wrote out an order for a Harper's Ferry musket that is supposed to be almost like new. It has been greased up and in a box since the Civil War. It cost me eight dollars and that is the most I ever paid for anything. It will be nice to play soldier with and to have for my museum.

From the International Trading Company I ordered three American Army helmets from the Great War. They cost me a dollar-and-a-half apiece. My friends and I will have fun wearing them when we play soldier.

Other times I have ordered stamps from the International Trading Company. I have many stamps in my album now. Sometimes I trade them with friends. Theron has the most and Baldy has some.

My ordering letters are ready to go now. Monday I will take them to the post office on the way to school. I will have to get money orders to pay for what I ordered. The post office is right beside the railroad track. There is a man who guards the crossing and holds up a sign that says "stop" so people will know not to drive or walk in front of a train. Sometimes the train switches cars back and forth and it is a little hard to tell just what they are going to do next. The man with the sign keeps it safe for everyone.

I have been inside all day. I think I will put on my raincoat and go out and splash around a little. I will be sure to wipe my shoes when I come back in.

COASTER WAGON

Now I have a bump on my head and both hands hurt from where I hit the car and the ground. So I think I will tell about my wagon. It is a coaster wagon. That means when I kneel in it on one knee and use the other foot to push on the ground, I can get it to go fast enough so I can quit pedaling and coast. Anyway, it coasts downhill really well. I like it a lot and I use it all the time to haul things, to give my sisters rides and to pedal it fast. It has a tongue that comes back up so I can steer the wagon when I am in it or it can go out in front so I can pull the wagon.

Sometimes I tie my dog, Pal, to the wagon and get him to pull it, but that doesn't work very well. He goes wherever he wants to with the empty wagon. If I put anything in, he can't pull it.

Most of all I like to race my wagon downhill. We live at the bottom of a hill and at the top is the railroad station. I take my time pulling my wagon to the station. Then I head it downhill and get in on my left knee with my right leg outside to push or to help stop. There is a brake near the left rear wheel but it is just a stick fastened to the body so when I push forward on it the other end presses backward against the wheel. When I am going fast that is not enough, so I use my right foot on the sidewalk or ground.

There is sidewalk all the way down the hill to our house and up the next hill clear out to the Camp Ground. That makes it swell for riding the wagon and racing. It crosses two streets on the way down, but there are not very many cars.

This afternoon I took my wagon up to the station, turned it around and got in. Everything was just right. I pushed off and was going fast. The wind felt good in my face and it was fun to steer with the handle. I got across the first street all right and pushed with my foot to go faster. I was going as fast as I could and the wagon was bumping and rattling by the time I got to the second street.

There was a car coming, but I saw I could not stop and anyway I thought I could beat it to the crossing. I did, too, but it scared me a little and I turned to watch the car go by just behind me. When I looked, I accidentally turned the handle, or wagon-tongue, and steered the wagon off the sidewalk to the right.

Next thing I knew I hit a car parked in front of Mr. Harbach's house. The wagon went under the running board and it threw me into the car. My head hit first, then I lit on the ground. I got up and pulled my wagon back. It was all right except now it has a dent across the tongue where it hit the running board. Maybe I will have a dent in my head, too, after the bump goes down. I rode the wagon the rest of the way downhill and got some cold water from the pump for my head and my hands.

After things felt better I rode my wagon again, but I went toward the Camp Ground.

ERRAND
DOWNTOWN

This afternoon Mother asked me to go downtown to get some things for her. I like to do that. All she wanted was some steak and some prepared mustard and some black thread. I thought I could carry that without taking my wagon and it was a good day for walking. I went up the hill past Mr. Harbach's house, across the street and past the King sister's house. They are teachers and are friendly to kids. Then came the garage where Dr. Salter's hired man, Mr. Doll, works on cars and sells tires. Overhead is a Michelin tire sign that shows a man made out of tires. He is holding a candle and yawning and saying "Time to Retire."

Dr. Allen Salter has a big house on the corner. I don't think he is married or has any family, but he is a doctor like my dad. His father was a doctor here a long time ago. By the railroad tracks is the passenger station on one side and the big freight depot on the other. Across the tracks on the corner is the White Building where Dr. Salter has his office above the Lena State Bank. Dr. W. E. Tucker is a dentist and he has his office up there, too. The next one west is Leamon's Furniture Store, then Downing's Bakery, and then Clark's Blacksmith Shop.

Taylor's Grocery Store is one block east of the White Building, and the block between is the main part of town, even though there are other businesses on both sides of that and also on the north side of the tracks. My dad's office is above Taylor's Store right on the corner of the highway and Main Street. Before I went to the store I went up to Dad's office to get some money.

There are twenty steps up to the second floor and the second door on the left goes into his waiting room. On the outside, each of his big tall windows has L. O. Vickery, M.D., Physician and Surgeon in gold letters. By the stairway, outside, is a wooden sign he calls his shingle. It says the same thing in gold letters on black. His waiting room is large, with a high ceiling. There are chairs around three walls and there is a big oak library table in the middle. A coal stove in one corner heats water which goes to radiators in the other rooms. The ceilings are tin with patterns and are painted white. The floors are linoleum, worn at the doorways.

The door that opens to the inside office has a clock sign on it that tells when the doctor will be back if he is not there. If it is turned over it says "Doctor Is In." That is what it said. There were several people waiting. Some of them said, "Hello, Eugene." I said "Hello," too, but I didn't know for sure who they were. I went to the door and knocked. I felt a little embarrassed doing that, but Dad told me that was what I should do.

Pretty soon Dad came to the door and said, "Hi, Jack, what can I do for you?" I said, "Mother said I should get some money for groceries." He said, "OK, will this be enough?" He gave me two dollars and I thought that would be plenty and maybe I could get an ice cream soda, too. I said, "Thank you. 'Bye," and he said, " 'Bye, Jack."

I knew that the rest of the office had two big rooms. Each went clear across the building. The first one had a desk on the right where someone could work on the books to keep track of who paid and who owed money. He also kept patient records there. On the left there was a partly walled-off room where Dad had his laboratory shelf and microscope and a sink. On one side was a big static electricity machine that Dr. Krieder had used, but Dad did not think it helped much so he did not use it. He showed me how it worked, though. By turning big flat wheels it made electricity which jumped like little lightning bolts between two metal rods. A patient was supposed to hold onto handles and let the electricity go through him. Dad bought the office things and the practice from the doctor who set up the office in 1895.

The third big room was his main office and examining room. On the right going in, on the side next to the highway, was his big roll-top desk and his swivel chair. Just beyond that was a big iron safe. He can open and close the safe but he does not dare turn the knob because nobody knows the combination. It was Dr. Krieder's, too. Dad's examining chair is in the center of the room. On the other side is a partition separating off his drug room where he keeps his medicines. There is a sink for water and an electric plate where he can boil water to make digitalis tea for people with heart trouble. He mixes medicines and puts them in bottles or boxes or jars back there. Lots of times he just counts out pills or tablets from a stock bottle and puts them in an envelope with directions on it so the patient will know how to take them. Since it is summer, the big windows are open to let the air go back and forth. That is fine except when a train goes by and the coal smoke comes in.

Downstairs I went back to the meat department and told Mr. Taylor that Mother wanted a pound-and-a-half of round steak for Swiss steak. He cut it nice and even with a big knife and pounded it a little with a special hammer, then took slices of suet and laid them on the meat and cut them in with a knife. When he was through he wrapped it carefully in paper and gave it to me. "Here," he said, "that ought to taste good." I told him she also wanted a jar of prepared mustard and a spool of black thread. "Fine and dandy," he said. "Just a minute." He put them in a sack and said, "That will be eighty-five cents." I gave him a dollar. He gave me fifteen cents and said, "Thank you." I said, "You're welcome" and went out the door to the second store down the street.

That was Mr. Metz's store. He is the druggist and his store is a drug store. He has a nice big soda fountain and he makes the best chocolate ice cream sodas. I sat on a tall stool at the fountain and asked him for a chocolate soda. He asked if I wanted vanilla ice cream in it or chocolate. I thought a minute and then said, "Chocolate." It would not have made any difference. Both are so good it makes my mouth water to think about them. Sometimes, though, when it really does not make any difference what I decide, it takes longer to make up my mind.

I took plenty of time with the soda. Then I hiked back home. I cut across the railroad yards in between freight cars on the two sidings and over the main tracks. Everything was quiet. Sometimes when they are moving the cars or when a train is coming through we put a penny or a nickle on the track just to see how the train flattens them out. Sometimes we can't find them afterward, but usually we can. I have several of those in my collection. Back home Mother thanked me for doing the errand. I told her she was welcome and gave her the dollar I had left over. Then I worked on my stamp album for a while before supper.

SHOOTING FOR CASH

This afternoon was an exciting one for me. I had my first practice at target shooting with a rifle. Mr. Cash Eells is a good friend of my dad's. I have known him for a long time and I always like to talk to him. He has been to Mexico and he likes it down there, even though he was a soldier chasing a Mexican raider. He was a sergeant in the Seventh Cavalry of the United States Army. They were in Texas, near El Paso, when Pancho Villa and his soldiers came into the United States on a raid. Pancho Villa was trying to upset the government of Mexico. I guess he wanted to be president but couldn't get elected, so he started a revolution.

Our cavalry chased the Pancho Villa rebels back into Mexico. They did not catch him, but they made sure he didn't do that again. Mr. Eells had a chance to look around Mexico and he thought it was warm, pretty, interesting and had a great history. He hopes to go back someday and get better acquainted. He likes to study history and find out as much as he can, especially about things he feels close to. He knows a lot about the Seventh Cavalry and the Battle of the Little Big Horn in Montana in 1876. There Colonel George Armstrong Custer and about 250 Seventh Cavalry soldiers fought several times as many Sioux Indians under Chief Sitting Bull. All the soldiers were killed, but the Indians had to retreat toward Canada because more United States Cavalry soldiers came after them.

Mr. Eells likes to be called Cash and said it was all right for me to call him that. He has learned a lot about Chief Black Hawk and his Sac Fox Indians and the Black Hawk War. It seems he knows every move the Indians and soldiers made at Kellog Grove during the two battles there. That is about ten miles southwest of Lena. He also knows all sorts of interesting things about the history of Lena, like where the first brick house was and the first school, churches and inn.

When he was Sergeant Eells of the Seventh Cavalry, Cash became such a good marksman that he was given the assignment of teaching new soldiers how to shoot. He was an expert with a rifle, pistol, saber and machine gun. When our country got into the Great War, he thought he would get a chance to go overseas to fight in France. The army decided it would be better for him to stay in this country and teach recruits to shoot. So that is what he did, but he was disappointed that he did not get to France.

My friends and I have shot our air rifles or BB guns and most of us are pretty accurate. Dad thought it was time I learned how to shoot a .22-caliber rifle and do it right. On his birthday last March I gave Dad a Stevens .22-rifle and he has let me fire it a few times with him. He wanted Cash to teach me about gun safety and target shooting.

The Lena Rifle Club has an indoor range in the basement of the White Building downtown just south of the Illinois Central Railroad Station. The Lena State Bank is on the first floor right over the rifle range. It is an official fifty-foot indoor target range approved by the National Rifle Association. Our Lena Rifle Team is made up mostly of war veterans and they are really good. They win lots of matches with other teams in the midwest. Sometimes the teams go to each other's ranges and shoot "shoulder-to-shoulder." Other times they fire at home and exchange targets to see who won. Everything is very fair and done just according to the rules. Sometimes a hair's breadth tells who won, but there are standard ways to judge and they all stick to it.

Right after school, I met Cash at the rifle range. It is Friday, so I was out of school for a couple of days and his regular work was done for the week. He's a lineman for the telephone company and he often has to do extra work on Saturday or Sunday.

He said, "Hello, Eugene. Doc says you want to shoot a rifle. How much do you know about it?" I said, "Hello, Mr. Eells. Not very much, I guess. I have shot an air rifle a lot." He said, "Well, that's something. We'll start at the beginning. I have my Winchester target rifle here. I will demonstrate the parts of the rifle and its sling and explain them. Then we will talk about safety in the use of the rifle and the rules of the range."

There is much to learn. I did not get it all today. But it is so interesting and so much fun I can hardly wait till next week when he will see me again. He told me about the rifle, what each part is supposed to do, how to hold the rifle in the different positions to be sure it is pointed at the target, how to use the sling to steady the rifle and how to protect myself and everybody else. There is more to it than just loading and shooting.

He handles his rifle easily, even in the offhand or standing position. To me it is heavy and I feel like I am going to tip over when I aim it standing up. Kneeling and sitting positions are a little steadier, but still pretty wobbly. Prone is the best for me. That is lying down on the stomach, using the left arm in the sling to steady the rifle, with the left hand holding it and the right elbow to steady it on the right. The right hand holds the stock with the index finger on the trigger to squeeze off the shot whenever the sights are lined up just right. He used NRA paper targets and his own drawings to show me how the rear and front sights and the target are supposed to look when the gun is aimed correctly.

He showed me that, when a person is in a shooting position, there is a place where the rifle just naturally points. The trick is to adjust one's position until that natural point is the same as the target. Then the shooter changes the aiming until the sights look just right to him before he squeezes his right hand on the gunstock. Of course, when he squeezes nothing can actually move but the trigger finger and that is what makes the gun go off. There is always some quiver or wobbling, but if the shooter only closes the trigger hand when the gun is on target, whenever it fires, the bullet will hit the center of the target. If a person shoots several times and the bullet holes make a group close together, but not in the center of the target, the rear sight can be changed to put the group where it belongs. This is called "sighting in" the rifle.

On some rifles the rear sight cannot be moved. If a person finds his gun is shooting to one side or the other, he has to change his sighting to account for it. Cash said that is called "Kentucky windage," which is all right for rough shooting, but not good enough for careful target shooting.

Guns are dangerous. Everybody who uses one should understand how they work and how to keep them safe. There are several important rules about loading, unloading, carrying, crossing fences and so on. Cash says the main rule is "Never point the gun at anything you don't want to shoot." Another one that goes with that is "Never let anyone point a gun at you, even in fun, loaded or unloaded." He talked about safety and careful handling while he was showing me things about the gun.

He had me fire a few shots in each position, just to get the feel of it. It felt good. He explained about wincing, which means jerking a little just as the gun goes off, and canting, or holding the rifle slightly twisted instead of with the front sight straight up and down. He said he would teach me how to correct those. He helped me get into good prone position. Before we were through I fired five shots that were all in the counting part of the target, about the size of a quarter. They were not all in the middle, but they counted. He said it was very good for the first time.

I liked to have Mr. Eells teach me. He is serious about it and patient and he knows what he is doing. I liked the smell of the powder and the leather and the Hoppe's No. 9 gun oil, and the feel of the gun. It is exciting to line up the sights just right, hold the gun on target and then have the bullet hit right where I wanted it to go. It is very precise. So many little things can throw it off. That is why many trained marksmen can shoot in the same rifle match and one will be the best.

When I went out hunting with Dad and he let me shoot the Stevens rifle, I enjoyed being outdoors with him and shooting the rifle, but I did not like to kill the animals. I enjoy knowing how to be a good shot and how to use guns, but I would rather shoot at targets than hunt.

ART AND
THE SWORD

My good friend Art has moved away. I feel bad about it. His father is a Brethren minister, Reverend Wagner. He had lived in Lena for many years, but got a call from a church in Ohio and decided to move there. Art's name is Arthur, of course, but we always called him by his nickname. He was good in school and liked to ride a bike, hike, and do other things with us. Since his dad was the preacher, he always had to do more church things than we did. He lived in a big brick house that used to be a Brethren Church building and still has a half-round glass window up near the roof.

This spring Art and I were interested in stories about King Arthur and his Knights of the Round Table. We decided to make up a play about those times and get our friends to practice it and put it on for our families and anyone else who wanted to come. We kept the names King Arthur and Sir Lancelot for Art and me, but we invented everything else.

We thought we could get two other boys and two girls to be in it with us. We figured if we tried to have any more, they would not keep their minds on what we were doing and would just fool around.

The play was not very long. We started out with King Arthur in a crown and robe wearing a sword and sitting at a round table. Two knights, Aaron and Baldy, called Sir Ethelred and Sir Duncan, were also sitting at the table. King Arthur said, "Sir Lancelot has been gone a long time. I hope his quest was successful." Sir Duncan said, "He should be here for the meeting."

Right then I came in with armor on my chest, carrying a helmet and wearing my sword. I said, "Hail, King Arthur. I have carried out my quest. I killed the dragon and chased off a highwayman. But I discovered a lady in distress that I could not help. I need reinforcements."

Sir Ethelred said, "We hasten to your aid. What is the trouble?" Sir Duncan said, "Yes, we will help you. Do we need to bring our army?"

I said, "Twenty good men will do. Lady Agnes in her castle in the next duchy is held in thrall by the Black Knight and his henchmen." We three knights left the stage. King Arthur waved goodbye and said, "Fare thee well, noble knights. Justice and chivalry must prevail." Then the curtain closed.

We had a little trouble with that. We used a place in their yard, near where the new cheese factory is going to be built, for our stage. We strung a wire on poles across the front and borrowed a couple of old curtains from Art's mother for our stage curtain. Pulling it back and forth was tricky.

We hurried to change the scenery on our outdoor stage. We carried off the furniture except for one chair for Lady Agnes, who was really Mary Agnes who lived almost next door, to stand on. We quickly put her castle around her. It was made out of cardboard and by standing on the chair she could look over the top wall.

When the curtain opened again, she was looking toward her left, very distressed, as if she were hoping for help. In front of her castle was the Black Knight in his black armor and sword. Actually, it was Virgene, so it was her armor and sword. We three knights came on stage and the Black Knight said, "Stop where you are. Lady Agnes is my prisoner until she gives me her treasures. My army will destroy you."

I said, "We are not afraid. We have twenty men whose hearts are true and we will prevail. We will lay siege to the castle." Then the Black Knight went behind the castle wall and we went to different places as if we were surrounding the castle.

Art's mother was helping. She pulled the curtain across very carefully, waited a few minutes, then opened it again. King Arthur came to the center of the stage. He said, "A week has gone by. Can you not take this castle?" Lady Agnes stuck her head up and said, "Help me. Help me." The Black Knight stuck his (her) head up and said "Go away. You can never win."

King Arthur said, "I will lead you in the attack. We will prevail." Then his mother pulled the curtain across the stage. We yelled and hit our swords and made noise like a battle for a while.

Then the curtain opened again. King Arthur's knights marched the Black Knight off stage at sword's point. Lady Agnes came out of the castle and said, "Thank you, noble knights and King Arthur."

King Arthur said, "Right and justice will prevail in my kingdom." That was all. The curtain was closed and the wire fell down.

Counting our parents and various brothers and sisters there were twelve or fifteen people watching us. We thought it was fun. They clapped and everything. Some of the mothers had brought some lemonade and cookies. It seemed like a picnic. We were all excited and laughing.

We had made our armor and helmets and the castle out of big cardboard boxes from Leamon's Furniture Store. After we had cut things out we used crayons, water colors and paint to make them look more realistic. What we wore we tied on with strings. Our costumes and castle weren't very good, I guess, but they lasted through the play. We all used our imaginations.

The only things that were real were King Arthur's and Sir Lancelot's swords. Art and I made them of wood. We drew pencil lines on a board and sawed them out to make a good handle and guard and blade. After the play, we threw away all the other props and gave Art's mother back her table, chairs and curtains.

We kept our swords because they meant a lot to us. When Art moved away, I gave him my sword and he gave me his.

MY SHACK

I think I will write about my shack. Way last summer or fall, some of my friends and I were having fun back in the woods beyond the chicken house. It is a long area that comes to a point and there are different sizes of trees. There are different kinds, too. It is not really much of a woods, but it is shaded and we like to play in it. We don't bother the chickens or ducks very much. Sometimes we find a nest where a duck hen has hidden it. If there are any old eggs that did not hatch, we throw them against a fence post to hear them pop. Then they smell pretty bad, but it goes away after a rain or two.

That day we had our BB guns and were shooting at targets we put up, sometimes a piece of wood or a leaf or piece of paper. We could usually hit the targets because we practiced. Part of the time we pretended to be Indians. We walked very quietly in single file and crouched down so we would not be seen. Whenever one of us saw something to shoot at, he would sight quickly and shoot and then go back to hiding behind a tree or bush.

Then we decided to be pioneers and fight the Indians off. I thought if we were going to be pioneers and settlers, we should have a fort. Baldy thought so too and so did Woody and Aaron. We picked out a place beside the farthest back fence where there were some trees we could use for corner posts. We didn't cut the trees down, we just used them where they were. Our fort was not very square.

We scattered out to find some boards and nails and a hammer and saw. Some of the things were hard to find. We did not do it all at once. One day we got boards all the way around the bottom except for a place for the door. Another day when we found a board we put it on someplace. Different fellows worked on it. I think Barton and Dale and Willard helped at times. Maybe Aaron's brother Rusty came sometimes when Aaron was supposed to look after him. He's not as big as the others.

We played out there every once in a while and the fort gradually was built. By the time snow came we had boards across the top for a roof. Quite a bit of snow and rain came through anyway. We had a couple of boards for a door but we did not have any hinges. We just moved the door back and forth. We had rifle slits in the walls instead of windows. They were just open and big enough to stick our air rifles through and aim them.

It took a lot of work to build the fort, but we had a good time. For all the work, it really was not very big. Three of us could be inside at once and it was not too bad, but if four of us went in we bumped into each other. We thought we had to have a roof, but it was more fun before we put the roof on. We kept bumping our heads on it.

We tried to make a little table to go inside. It was wobbly and small and not much use. After we put the roof on we couldn't see very well inside, either. We just went in when it was good daylight and light came through the cracks. We pretended a lot, though, and fought some good battles shooting out of our rifle slits at wild Indians who were attacking our fort.

When winter came we did not go out to the fort. It stayed there all right. Snow piled up on it and around it, but it did not fall down. Early this spring Baldy and I went out to see it and check it out. It was there, but it seemed so small we were disappointed. Maybe we grew a little, but it was not as big as we remembered.

One day my dad went out with me to look at it while he was feeding the chickens and I was gathering eggs. He said, "Jack, you and your friends ought to have a bigger shack than that. It would give you a place of your own, sort of a headquarters." I thought that would be wonderful, but I told him, "We tried to build it as big as we could, but we couldn't find very good boards. And we're not very good builders either, I guess."

Dad said, "That would be a good project for me. I did a lot of carpentering. It wouldn't be too hard."

The next thing I knew, in just a few days, Dad brought some new boards and two-by-fours and nails and got out his hammer and saw and something he called a spirit level and went to work. He asked me where I wanted it. We picked out a place not far from our fort where there was more open space. He laid it out to be eight feet wide and ten feet long.

He put heavy boards underneath to hold the floor and walls and also to serve as skids if we ever wanted to move it.

He did not have much time at home to work on it, just early mornings and evenings while it was still light. Sometimes my friends and I were there to watch and if there was anything we could hold or carry to help, we did. He got the frame up and a roof covered by tar paper and real working windows and a door. It was all pine wood, inside and out, and it was wonderful.

Baldy and I have slept in it overnight already. We just put blankets on the floor. We rolled up part of our clothes for a pillow. At first the blankets under us seemed soft enough, but during the night the floor felt pretty hard. I think we will figure out something softer to lie on next time. We made a little camp fire out in front and Mother showed us how to fry bacon and eggs in a skillet over the fire. Then she mixed some pancake batter and we fried them in the bacon grease. That was really good.

Some day we will have a stove inside the cabin, with a stove pipe for a chimney, Dad said, and maybe an army cot if we want it. He is building a table, and I'll bet it won't be wobbly.

The old fort is still there, but it does look like a shack. The new one is so nice, it looks like a cabin. It is ours and we will have meetings in it and keep things in it. It will be our headquarters. We are still going to call it "The Shack," though.

BRINGING
BOXER HOME

This was one of the happiest days I ever had. School has finished for the year and the weather is sunny and warm, but what I am so happy about is Boxer. He is my new horse. He really is a horse, but not a tall one like Cactus. Dad's horse is tan or buckskin color. Mine is white with big black spots and just a little brown. Out west they might call him a "paint."

He is really nice and I have to look after him, feed him, curry him, water him and clean out his stall. He is in the box stall in our little barn where Cactus used to be. Mr. Gillette, who helps Dad, lives across town and has a small barn also. He is taking care of Cactus there now. Mr. Gillette used to be a farmer. He is retired and lives in town. He would not have to work at all, but he and Dad are good friends and Mr. Gillette likes "to have something to do." We all like him. He is like a grandfather, but Dad calls him Bill.

We spent the whole day bringing Boxer home and that is why I am so tired tonight. Dad had been looking for a horse for me and he found one that he thought would be about the right size on a farm near Willow. That is about ten miles away, I think. I was really excited when he told me about it. I asked Baldy and Louis if they would help me bring him home. They said, "Sure," so early this morning Dad drove us and my bicycle and his saddle over to the farm.

Dad paid sixty dollars for Boxer and then we put the bridle and blanket and saddle on him for the trip home. I rode him first, Baldy rode my bike and Louis walked. The trouble was, Boxer did not want to leave his barn and his farm. He walked around the yard, but I just couldn't make him go out and down the road. Dad said, "He doesn't like to leave home. Lots of horses are like that. Here, I'll help." He took hold of the bridle and led Boxer out of the barnyard and a little way down the road. I kept the reins in my hands. "There," Dad said, "he should go where you tell him now." Dad stayed with us in the car for another half mile or so. We were getting along fine, so he drove back to Lena to go to work.

We did not go back to town on the main highway. We stayed on gravel roads. It was dusty, but there were not very many cars and we felt safer. We crossed U.S. 20 at the Tiger Whip schoolhouse corner. The school is a neat old stone country schoolhouse. I don't have any idea why they call it that. We kept going north until we came to the Howardsville Road, then we turned east.

Every once in a while, we stopped to rest or to look around. The first time we stopped Boxer had to relieve himself. There was alot of splashing, and it surprised us, but he probably felt better. About every mile we changed around. The fellow on the bicycle got the horse, the one hiking got the bike, and the horse rider walked. The saddle was Dad's McClellan saddle which he said was designed by a Civil War general. I suppose they are easy to make and not very heavy, but they are hard to sit on. I thought I was going to have bruises and blisters on my bottom and the other guys did, too.

Once in a while someone in a farmyard or a field waved at us. We waved back. I suppose we were a strange parade. We were hot and happy. It was the middle of the afternoon before we reached home. We all went right for the pump and drank a lot of cold water. I filled a bucket for Boxer and he drank quite a bit of it.

Mother said, "I'll bet you are starved. It has been a long time since breakfast." I tied Boxer to a tree and we all went in the house. Mother fixed us peanut butter and jelly sandwiches and cookies and milk. We were so hungry we didn't talk at all. We just ate. We thought we would be back before noon, so we did not take anything to eat. Whenever we stopped along the way, Boxer ate some grass. He was not as bad off as the rest of us.

We took Boxer in the barn and let him look around his new home, then brought him back out for a few rides around the block. Virgene and Thelma and Aaron and Russell came over to look and, of course, my sisters Virginia and Margery were excited, too.

Mother looked him over very carefully and said, "My, what a nice horse. You will have to take good care of him." Most of the kids did not want to ride Boxer right away. They wanted to get used to him first. Aaron rode a little and Virgene said she would tomorrow. Baldy and Louis and I felt like old cowboys showing the others how to do it.

When everybody went home to supper, I led Boxer into his stall and took off his saddle, blanket and bridle. He shook himself and stomped on the straw and started looking around. I put a can of oats in the built-in open box where he could eat it, then I climbed up into the haymow and pitched some hay into his manger. He was sweating, so I rubbed him down with a gunny sack but didn't curry him.

After supper I went back out to see him and give him some more water. He was quiet and watching. He liked it when I rubbed his cheeks and nose and ears. His nose seems more square on the end than most horses' noses. He turns his ears different ways to catch all the noises around his new home.

Dad went out to see him. He patted Boxer on the rump and neck and rubbed his nose and told him he was a good horse. Dad seemed happy and I sure was. I hope I can take good care of Boxer. I think we will be friends and go on rides in the country together.

FAMILY CAMP

We just got back from a family trip. It is the middle of the summer vacation. Dad and Mother wrote to Aunt Harriett and Uncle Otto in Indiana and they figured out how to get the two families together for a camping vacation and visit. There is a camping place in Pilcher Arboretum near Joliet that is about a hundred miles from here. It is a little farther than that from Fairmount, Indiana, but Uncle Otto said that was all right. They got in their car and we got in ours and we drove to Pilcher Arboretum for a three-day camp.

We could not possibly get into the Model T Ford roadster that Dad drives on calls. He got it from Dr. Krieder when he bought the office things and it is a good car. He taught me how to drive it, but I can't take it by myself. Just this spring Dad bought a new car. It is a Dodge sedan and we can all get in it, Mother and Dad in front and Virginia, Margery and I in the back seat. It is a good strong car and can go up over High Point without shifting into second. It is pretty, too. It has curtains on the back windows and glass vases on the inside for flowers. Out in front over the radiator it has a round enameled Dodge medallion with a star in it and it has a thermometer to tell how hot the water is in the radiator. It starts from inside. Dad doesn't have to go out in front to crank it like he does the Ford. It has a gear shifting stick and I already know how to work it, putting in the clutch and everything. Dad has let me drive it a little, but not by myself.

Dad bought a big twelve-by-fourteen-foot canvas tent with poles and stakes and he got army cots for us to sleep on. Mother fixed up food in baskets and lemonade in thermos bottles. She said there had to be a grocery store where we could get things we needed to eat. It was so warm we did not need to take very much to wear. Dad packed everything in the trunk and on the running boards. He said, "Maybe we should have a trailer." Then we left.

The road was paved all the way to Joliet. That made it easier to ride. We had the windows open because it was so hot. Dad just loved to drive the new car. He speeded it up to forty miles an hour. Mother saw that on the speedometer and she said, "Otis, twenty miles an hour is fast enough. We don't want any accidents." Dad said, "Oh Grace, it handles just as well at forty as at twenty." After that he drove thirty most of the time.

When we reached Joliet we followed a map and road signs to find the arboretum. It was a beautiful big wooded park. It had all different kinds of trees in it and they had little signs to tell what kind they were. At the camping ground they had a water hydrant for drinking water and two big shower houses and bathrooms for men and women.

Pretty soon the Rigsbee's came in. It was very exciting. Mother and Aunt Harriett are sisters and Dad and Uncle Otto are old friends. My cousin Marthene is just my age and I was extra glad to see her, but I like her older sisters Lavelda and Clarice, too. They all play baseball. We had fun at that. We looked around while Dad and Uncle Otto were getting things out of the cars.

Then we helped set up the tents. We held up the poles while the men drove in the stakes and tightened the ropes. First thing we knew, there were our tent homes. I helped Dad open up the cots and put them where they belonged. We rolled up the tent walls right away to let the breezes in. Mother put sheets and a blanket on each cot. She said it would get cool during the night.

There were stone and iron stoves or fireplaces that Mother and Aunt Harriett could use for cooking. Before long Dad built a fire in one of the stoves and sort of hinted that he hoped it would not be too long till supper. Aunt Harriett had brought some chickens all cleaned and ready to cook. So it really was not very long till we had fried chicken, fried potatoes, bread and jam and lemonade for supper. It sure tasted good.

It was still light enough for us to walk down paths and look around some more before bedtime, but mostly we talked and enjoyed being together. We don't get to see each other very often. When it was dark we went to bed. Each family had a lantern, but we really did not use them much. The folks thought it would be daylight early and that we should go to bed and get our rest and be ready for it. I was not sure I could sleep on the hard cot and with so many things to think about. But I guess I did. At least I did not know much until it was daylight again.

Our mothers fixed oatmeal and brown sugar breakfasts. Then the kids went for hikes in the woods. I guess Virginia and Margery stayed near the folks but the rest of us went down into a ravine and across a creek and all through the big woods. It was a clean woods, but there were bushes and small trees in some places. It was peaceful and there were lots of different birds and many squirrels, gophers and chipmunks.

After lunch back at the camping place we played some work-up baseball using my bat and softball. Then we ran around awhile and hiked some more in the woods. The shower felt good after being hot all day. For supper Mother and Aunt Harriett had fried steak and potatoes and Dad and Uncle Otto had found ice cream somewhere. It was all mighty good.

In the evening we sang a while and talked and then turned in for a good sleep. The next morning was our last day together. We did about the same things—hiked, played games, talked, ate together. Then we took down the tents and packed everything back in the automobiles. We were sad at leaving, but mostly we were glad we could be together and hoped we could do it again.

It took us four or five hours to get home. We were tired, too. Mother and Dad unpacked and put things away. I helped a little. But soon after supper we were all ready to go to sleep and happy to crawl into our own beds.

BLACK TOOTH

I guess I am going to have a black tooth, or at least a grey one. I don't like it very much; it is right in front on top on the left. But at least I still have a tooth there, even if it is chipped a little. Last week was warm enough but it was rainy. It was not any fun to ride. I didn't take Boxer out of his big square stall for exercise. About Friday Dad said, "He will get fractious if you don't take him out for exercise." I was not exactly sure then what he meant, but I think I know now.

I called Aaron to come over. He is a nice guy, taller than I am, blond, slender and plays the violin. He has to practice a lot, but sometimes he can come to play with the rest of us. When he got here, I said, "Let's saddle up Boxer and ride him. He needs the exercise. It's not raining now." Aaron said, "Okay!" Boxer was a little jumpy, but we got the bridle, saddle blanket and saddle on. I said I would ride first because he had not been ridden for a while, but Aaron should hold the bridle till I got settled in the saddle.

When I get on I have to put my left foot up real high to reach the stirrup, then I pull myself up by holding the saddle horn and jumping. Dad ordered a regular western saddle for me from Montgomery Ward and Company, so I don't use his McClellan saddle anymore.

Well, I was jumping up to sit in the saddle when Aaron yelled, "He's laying his ears back!" Then he let go of the bridle. Boxer jerked his head down and bucked his back up in the air. That boosted me up. When I came down I lit on some part of the saddle but doubled over so my face hit the saddle horn. He bucked me up again and I couldn't get hold of anything. When I came down I struck him, but fell on down to the ground beneath his belly. He hit me with his rear hooves when he jumped over me. Then he went bucking back to the barn, went into his stall, turned around and kicked his manger, then ran out past us and across the street, through Leckington's flower bed and on down the street east. I think that is what Dad meant by fractious.

Dad came home about that time. He jumped in his car and drove around the block to head off the horse. Pretty soon he came back, leading Boxer. He locked him in the stall and then looked us over. We tried to fix up the flower beds but you could still tell something had happened to them.

My face hurt, my tooth was the worst, and I had a little bruise on my right hip. Aaron wasn't hurt. Later on I took Boxer out and walked him for exercise and he was quiet. I guess he just had to get it out of his system. I nailed the boards back on his manger.

Mother and Dr. Alzeno talked it over about my tooth and they decided to leave it in and see what happens. He said if I didn't lose it, it would get dark and maybe I would want to have it out anyway. That was several days ago and it is getting dark already, but I would rather keep it if I can.

GRANDFATHER HAWKINS

Grandfather and Gramma Hawkins came to visit last week. Gramma is sweet and quiet and not very big and she seems just like a grandmother. Everybody likes her and at home she always has cookies or something that kids like. She teaches Sunday school and helps Grandfather. He is a Wesleyan Methodist minister and they live in Marion, Indiana.

They also have a cottage on the Methodist Camp Grounds at Fairmount, Indiana. Mother and I visited them there during camp meeting when I was little and we lived in Fairmount. We lived in a house Grandfather owned. I was born in another house of Grandfather's in Fairmount. When we went out to the Camp meeting it was very hot and the flies bothered me. They had long meetings and I got tired, but the singing was fun. My mother and Gramma were good singers. Grandfather, who is Mother's father, of course, was usually up on the platform of the tabernacle with the other preachers. Sometimes he preached, and people got up from the long hard benches and walked to the railing down in front. That was the altar where they knelt down and prayed and decided they wanted to be Christians and have Jesus Christ be their Lord and Savior. Grandfather was very serious about it, but Gramma fried the chicken and mashed the potatoes and made the gravy and all the other good things we had to eat in the cottage in between meetings. My Dad was away in medical school most of that time.

When they visited us in Lena, Grandfather was not preaching and I found it could be fun to talk to him, too. He told my sisters and me about their early life in Indiana when he was a farmer and a stock buyer. That meant he traveled by horse and wagon in southern Indiana and bought and sold cows, horses, mules and other farm animals. It was hard to make a living.

His whole name is Hiram Thomas Hawkins and he was born near Effingham, Illinois, where his father and mother lived. His father's name was Thomas Conover Hawkins and he was a preacher, too, but he also ran a sawmill and was a farmer.

Before he went to school to become a minister, Grandfather had a farm along Flatrock River. That is near Shelbyville, Indiana, and their house was a log cabin. That is where my mother was born. She just loved it because it was pleasant and peaceful and she liked all the farm animals.

After Grandfather became a minister, the family moved to different towns where he was the preacher for a few years at a time. One of the towns was Boxley, Indiana, and that is where she met my dad. They went to high school together.

Mother was a brown-haired girl with blue eyes. She was nice-looking, a good student and had a beautiful voice for singing. She and her older sister, my Aunt Harriett, were a lot alike. They were good friends. Grandfather was busy, but he must have paid attention. He said, "Otis Vickery was a lively, hard-working farm boy, but he played tricks and got into mischief in school. His father was a good farmer and his grandfather was a good doctor. Otis played football, but what I remember is that he won the temperance oratory contest. He and Grace (my Mother) were good friends all through school. He was supposed to do the class will for the graduating class and he did it in poetry."

Grandfather was glad when they were married and when Dad decided to go to the seminary to study to be a minister. I know that Dad wanted to be a medical missionary to Africa. He became a minister and a doctor, but by the time he finished all that study, he was pretty old and had a family. He never got to Africa, only to Illinois.

Mother was talking about those days, too, and I thought it was interesting to listen. She and Grandfather would remind each other of things, like how bad she felt when Grandfather shaved off his mustache. She was about ten years old and she thought he didn't look right without it. She cried. She liked to wade in Flatrock River and to go to the big woods up the hill from the barn.

They told how Aunt Harriett and Otto Rigsbee were good friends in high school and the four of them went places and attended parties together. Aunt Harriett and Uncle Otto were married first and went

to live on a farm near Fairmount. They had two
daughters, Lavelda and Clarice. About two weeks after
I was born, they had their third daughter. She was
Marthene and they always called us the twin cousins.

Dad took Grandfather and Gramma everywhere
around here in our Dodge sedan. The roads are all
good now and the weather is warm and sunny. They
went to Freeport to see the nice houses and where
Mr. Lincoln and Judge Douglas had one of their
debates near the Brewster House Hotel and to
McConnell and Winslow to see the Pecatonica River
and out to Kellogg Grove to see the Black Hawk
Monument.

One evening Dad took all of us to the Angelos
Restaurant in Freeport for a nice dinner. They said
Margery and Virginia are pretty little to go to a
restaurant, but they had a good time. Mr. Angelos
brought a high chair for Margery and she was happy
with her hamburger. She did not mess it up much.
Virginia had hamburger, too, but she sat in a chair
and her face was about level with the table. Mother
and Dad helped them. I had a veal cutlet. I like that
and I can cut the meat by myself. Gramma thought
it was nice to eat out and have something she or
Mother did not have to fix. Grandfather liked it, too.
He has a good appetite. That is what Mother says.
He was afraid it was too expensive, though. Dad told
him not to worry about it, just enjoy it, because Dad
was glad they came.

Grandfather asked the blessing before we started
to eat. He always does that no matter where he is.
One thing I noticed, it did not take as long as when
we are at home. In the morning he takes time for

study of some Bible verses that he calls morning devotion. He likes to have the breakfast all ready and then he takes a Bible verse for a text and prays a long prayer about that while the food gets cold. When Mother has made hot oatmeal and pancakes and sausages, she thinks he could do his devotions some other time, but he does it when he wants to.

One thing I like at Angelos' is that sometime in the meal they bring us little dishes of sherbet. It is cool and fresh and makes a person feel better for the rest of the meal. Mr. Angelos says we can enjoy the flavors of the dinner better after sherbet. It is not dessert. We have that afterward.

When we were all through and Margery was wiggling to get down, Grandfather told a story about a man that used to come to their house when they lived on the farm. He was a good friend, but he had never had a chance to go to school. Just the same, he liked to use big words even if he was not sure what they meant. After a big dinner, they asked him if he would like some more helpings. He patted his stomach and said, "Oh no. I have had the greatest of sufficiency, my wants are all saponified. If I ate any more, I would be flippity-floppity." Grandfather said that was how he felt.

On Saturday Dad took the day off to drive us all to Dubuque. Grandfather and Gramma had never seen the Mississippi River. Gramma did not say much, but Grandfather really wanted to go. He had seen the Ohio River and he had hoped to see the great Mississippi. Dad, Gramma and Grandfather sat on the front seat. Mother, Virginia, Margery and I were in back. It was warm and bright with blue sky and big soft white clouds. We rolled all the windows down.

The scenery seemed to be more beautiful as we went west. Beyond Stockton and around Woodbine and Elizabeth the hills were so high and valleys so green and pretty we were all busy looking and pointing and trying to get everyone to see everything. Dad stopped a couple of places so we could look across the valleys and woods and see all the black and white cows eating the green grass. Grandfather could not get over how nice it looked, how fat the cows were and how tall the corn was, even in hilly ground. He was farmer enough to know how good it was and preacher enough to thank God for everything.

In Galena we drove along Main Street. It is an old-fashioned town. Many buildings have been there since before the Civil War. They are older than Grandfather. He says, "I was born in '61, the year the war begun." That means the Civil War. Galena is full of things about the Civil War, like the DeSoto Hotel, the museum, and General Grant's home. We went to a little cafe and all had ice cream cones. Grandfather did not ask a blessing for them.

From Galena, Dad drove through the hills down to the valley of the Mississippi. When we reached East Dubuque we were at the edge of the river. Dad found a place near the bridge where we could see across the river to Dubuque. Grandfather looked and looked. Then he said, "The Father of Waters. The Mississippi River, the Father of Waters. I thank God I have been able to see it." It almost looked like there were tears in his eyes.

Soon Dad drove up on the bridge and across the river. It is high and a little scary, but we could see a long way up and down the river. We could see the city, with big houses up on the hills and cliffs and the business part along the river bank. Dad pointed out a statue on a hill just south of town. It was of Julien Dubuque, the founder of the city. On the waterfront was a tower which Dad said was a shot tower, where they dropped melted lead into water to make buckshot. At the end of the bridge, Dad paid money to a man because it was a toll bridge.

We drove around to look at the old churches and buildings. Then we stopped at a short, steep railway that goes right up the side of a cliff. They give rides on it for five cents apiece. Dad took all of us up except Mother and my sisters. She thought they would be scared. I wouldn't blame them. I was sort of scared, too. But when we were at the top of the cliff we could see all over. We looked awhile, then rode back down.

On the way home, we saw the same things. That makes it easier to remember.

While we were riding, Dad gave us some chewing gum. Grandfather would not take any. Dad asked him if he thought chewing gum was a sin.

Grandfather said, "I do not think it is a sin for you or other people to chew gum, but it would be a sin for me. You see, when I was a young man I chewed tobacco. When I was saved, I promised the Lord I would not chew tobacco any more. For me, chewing gum would just be a substitute for chewing tobacco."

DAD CALLS ME JACK

I knew Grandfather thought a lot about sin. Mother told me that Grandfather would wear neckties now, but when she was young he would not, because it was too showy and that meant a person was proud and it was a sin to be proud of things like that. He did not believe people should wear jewelry either. He even said wedding rings were jewelry and when he married Mother and Dad, he would not use a ring. Later Dad bought a gold ring for Mother because she wanted one.

Grandfather is a good man. He smiles and hugs and loves us. He has strict thoughts and he studies the Bible a great deal. He and Gramma went back to Indiana on the train on Sunday. Mother said it was a wonder he would travel on Sunday, but he had to be in Marion on Monday to lead a chapel service at the college. I am so glad they came and I hope someday we can go to visit them. They invited us.

PUP TENT

You wouldn't believe how neat my new pup tent is. It is not really new, of course. It is army surplus. But Dad bought it at an army-navy surplus store in Freeport and gave it to me, so it is new to me. That was two days ago, about noon. He said I was getting old enough to do some camping and here was a tent of my own. Maybe he said that because I have been talking about it since I saw a picture of a pup tent in a catalog last spring.

Baldy and I have slept overnight in my shack and we thought it would be fun to hike and camp other places. Dad must have thought so, too. When he gave me the package in our front yard, I tore off the paper and spread everything out on the ground. There were two big pieces of canvas that buttoned together to make the tent. The army made them that way so each soldier would only have to carry one-half of the tent, but when they camped he could team up with anybody and they would have a tent big enough for two men. The stakes, ropes and folding tent-poles were all there.

I was so happy and excited I started to put it up right away. Dad helped me and soon we had it up. It came to a center ridge about three feet high and spread out to the ground. It was big enough for Dad and me to crawl in, but we could not move around much. Two people could make beds with their blankets on the ground lengthwise and also put their other stuff inside it if they did not have too much. The tent could be buttoned way down to the ground if it was stormy, but usually the front would be left open to get in and out and only the pointed back be closed.

Stakes held the sides to the ground and Dad said I should always dig a little trench around just outside the walls. Then, if it rained the water could run off and not wet the ground inside the tent. I did not dig a trench in the yard, but went in the house to get Mother. I yelled, "Ma, come and look at my new tent!" She heard me before I got to the door.

She came out, all smiling. She said, "Oh my, that is a tent, isn't it. What are you going to do with it?" She looked at my dad as if she wondered what he was up to.

I said, "My friends and I will take hikes and carry our food and this tent. Then we will camp overnight."

She said, "Well, maybe you are big enough for that now. Just pick out a safe place to camp."

I said, "Can I call Baldy right away?" We will plan a camping hike and make out a list of what we need."

Dad said, "That sounds like a good idea. Plan it out and I will go over your list with you this evening. Now, I have to get to the office."

I left the tent up and went to call Baldy. He rode over on his bicycle and thought it was a great tent. Virginia and Margery crawled in it and went all around it. They thought it was nice, too.

Baldy said he would bring his Boy Scout hatchet with the belt sheath and his hunting knife and some matches. I said I would bring my Boy Scout mess kit and canteen. We asked Mother about food. She said we shouldn't load ourselves down with too many things, but how about weenies and buns, pork and beans and potatoes for our supper, and bacon, eggs and pancakes for breakfast? She said she would put in some apples to eat whenever we wanted to. We thought that would be just fine.

I wrote it all down after Baldy left and in the evening Dad looked it over and said, "This looks good to me, Jack. Where are you going? Will you hike or ride your bikes? Your blankets, tent and water will be rather heavy, but I think you and Don can carry it if you distribute it right." He calls Baldy "Don" because his first name is Donald. His last name is Baldwin. He calls me Jack just because he wants to, I guess.

I said, "We think we would like to hike and take our time. Maybe we will go to the Montague place. We like that."

The next day was Friday, warm and sunny with fluffy clouds. Baldy came right after dinner and we started packing our things. He rode over, but parked his bike in the barn because we wanted to walk this time. He is bigger than I am and probably stronger, but we divided things up as evenly as we could. He had his hunting knife and a Marble's waterproof matchbox in his pocket. I wore my hunting knife, too, and had my Boy Scout knife. We both had knapsacks that we got from the Boy Scout supply catalog.

Mother measured out pancake flour in a sack and gave us apples, wieners, buns, potatoes, bacon, eggs and a can of beans. We packed these and my mess kit and the tent stakes in the knapsacks, then tied our blankets, tent halves and poles around the outside. I filled my army canteen with water from the pump and fastened it on my belt. Ma asked us if we would like peanut butter and jelly sandwiches for an afternoon snack and we said, "You bet." She made those and wrapped them in oil paper and put them in the top of our knapsacks. We said, "Thanks," and took off across Downing's yard to Lena Street. She said, "You look like real outdoorsmen. Be careful now."

The pack was heavier than I thought it would be, but I could carry it. As we walked along, the straps hurt my shoulders so much I put my handkerchief under it on one side and stuck a bunch of leaves and grass under the other side. Later, I carried it in my hands part of the time. It is three miles or so northwest of town to the old Montague house. We took our time and stopped to rest every little while. Sometimes we put our packs down and waded in a creek or walked around in a pasture or a woods.

Finally we made it to the Waddams creek valley where the old stone house is, but we did not go up to the house. We went along the creek east and over a hill to a level place that we thought would be good for a camp. We had been there before and liked to hike in the valley and climb the bluffs and wade in the stream.

It was a hot day and we were really sweated up. The first thing we did was button our tent together and pitch it and put our blankets and other things inside. We didn't dig a ditch around it because we did not think it would rain, and anyway it would be too hard on Baldy's hatchet to dig with it.

As soon as we had our camp set up we took off our pants and shirts and went wading and splashing in the creek. It felt so good. We got wet all over and it was cool and fun. We found some frogs, but didn't try to catch them. There were fish in the creek and they would hurry to swim out of our way. I found a crayfish and picked it up to show Baldy. He said, "They are supposed to be good to eat, but they don't look very good."

I said, "I don't know how to fix them. I'll just let it go." He looked around the rocks in the water for more of them but just found bloodsuckers and bugs.

When we were cooled off we walked around in the sun to dry off, then put our clothes back on. I said I was hungry and Baldy said, "Hey, we didn't eat our sandwiches yet." So we did, right away, and they felt good in our stomachs.

We hunted for dry sticks and limbs for our fire and Baldy chopped them to sizes we could use. I whittled a couple of forked sticks to put in the ground on each side of our fire and a long stick to rest on them and go across the fire to hold the little kettle for boiling water to cook our potatoes. I also cut some long sticks for roasting the weenies.

We both whittled dry shavings for the middle of our fire to start it and had other sticks close by to feed the fire as it took hold. Baldy said he wanted to start the fire because he had the matches.

He did a good job. After the shavings caught fire, he put on more and more sticks till we had a bigger fire than we needed. The smoke blew around with a little breeze. It didn't always stay the same way. Pretty soon our eyes were full of smoke and we were coughing, but it was fun. I filled the kettle with water from the creek and managed to get it on the stick over the fire. We did not want to drink the creek water because cows used it, but we thought it would be all right for boiling potatoes. He cut them up and dropped the pieces in the water and I put the lid on the kettle.

I used the can opener blade of my knife to open the can of beans and stabbed my hand a couple of times doing it, but it didn't hurt much. Mother had put in an extra pie tin plate, cup, knife, fork and spoon because the mess kit only had one set. I dumped the beans, about half on each plate, and set the plates on the ground. We speared weenies on the sticks and held them over the fire. Pretty soon they fizzled and popped and dripped on the fire and we were ready to eat them. The beans were all right cold, but the potatoes were not cooking at all.

Baldy tried to build up the fire to help the water boil, but he bumped the kettle and it started to swing. I grabbed the stick to try to steady it, but the other end came off the forked support. So the kettle fell into the fire, its lid came off, and the water put the fire out. Smoke and ashes went into everything, our eyes, on the wieners and in the beans.

It was a mess. The first thing we did was pull our plates to one side and try to blow the ashes and burnt wood off the beans. We decided to eat the beans and weenies anyway because we were hungry and see what we could do with the potatoes after they cooled. The buns were all right. The beans were a little gritty, but they tasted good to us. When we could pick up the potatoes we ate them the way they were, which was just about raw. We had a couple of weenies left. We ate them without trying to warm them up. There were a few embers left of the fire, but we didn't have to worry about it getting out of control during the night.

We did not try to build up the fire again, but sat near it and talked and looked at all the colors of the sunset and then at the stars. The stars were bright and seemed close. We knew how to find the Big Dipper and the Little Dipper and the North Star. There were so many others. We didn't know what to call them, but it was really nice to look all over the sky and see the stars that were really so far away and seemed so close.

I heard a funny snuffling noise and looked around. Behind us were several cows who had walked up. They were just curious, but we were afraid they would step on things and put cow pies on our camp. We chased them away.

We were tired and it was good and dark. We took our shoes off, but did not undress to go to bed. We each rolled up in a blanket and used a folded-up knapsack for a pillow. I didn't know whether I could go to sleep, but I must have, because I woke up when I heard a barking noise outside the tent.

I threw off the blanket and jumped up, which was not the right thing to do, because I hit the tent and pulled loose some stakes. I ducked down again and got outside through the front of the tent, but knocked down the pole. By that time Baldy was awake and the tent was down all over him. He yelled out, "What is going on?" I told him I heard a fox or a dog and was trying to find it. He thrashed around under the tent trying to get out and saying things he was not supposed to say. I pulled his side of the tent up to help him get out and loosened up the stakes on that side. By the time he got out we did not have any tent left up. There wasn't any dog or fox, either.

After he got through being disgusted with me for wrecking the tent, we both laughed about it. There was good moonlight by that time and it was not long before we had the tent up again and our blankets straightened out. It was such a beautiful night we thought we would sit outside for a while. We were just sitting there when an owl, just as quiet as could be, swooped down from the cliff toward the hill. It was hunting and it went way down to the ground. There was a little fuss and a tiny squeal and the owl flew up and away. Baldy said, "He got a field mouse."

I said, "I guess so. How could he see that well?" We agreed owls must have better eyes for dark than we do, but they can't go out in the daylight. I would rather go out in the daylight.

We sat quietly, looking at the stars and getting sleepy again. All of a sudden Baldy whispered, "Look, up on the hill. It's a fox!" I looked hard and soon saw him on a part of the hill where the cows had eaten the grass down low. The light was good enough so we could see his bushy tail and even see that he was looking at us. "Let's chase him," I said. "That is what I heard from the tent."

The fox just stood still and watched us. We ran toward him and when we got to where we could see him real well, he turned and ran farther up the hill. Then he stopped and looked at us again, as if he wanted us to run after him. We ran some more and he ran ahead. By the time we got to the top of the hill he had gone off into tall grass or to the trees. We could not see him anywhere. We stood and panted for a while and looked up to see the bright moon and more stars. With brighter moonlight the stars did not show up so well, but there were lots of them.

Then we walked back to camp. The ground and rocks and stubble hurt our feet because we did not have our shoes on. When we ran up the hill we were too excited to notice.

Finally we got back into our blankets. It was wet with dew and a little chilly outside, but inside it was snug and warm. We slept until the sun came up and nothing happened except for a little grinding and rustly noise that woke me up once. In the morning I found a mole hill running under our tent about where my head had been. That was probably what I heard.

We got up and stretched and walked around. When we put on our shoes they were wet from the dew because they had been knocked out of our tent when it came down and we did not think to put them back in.

DAD CALLS ME JACK

We had plenty of sticks to make a new fire. I took the frying pan from the mess kit, put the bacon in it and held it over the fire. Baldy used the kettle to mix the pancake flour with some creek water. As soon as the bacon was done, I put the strips on a plate and broke the eggs into the bacon grease. After I fried the eggs there was enough grease left so we could fry the pancakes, too. Pretty soon everything was done. We put the eggs and bacon on the pancakes and ate it all. It took us quite a while to do all that, but the sun was not up very far.

At the creek we washed up the cooking and eating equipment. While it dried we shook out our blankets and tent halves. Then we packed everything back in and around the knapsacks, but we didn't put them on. We left them in the forks of two trees while we hiked downstream.

We went back and forth across the creek and looked for dragonflies and birds and frogs and fish. There were squirrels, gophers, ground hogs and chipmunks. The big Holstein cows were always around, too. Finally, we decided to head for home. Our packs were lighter, but still heavy enough. We took our time walking back to town. It was a nice day and we could always find something to look at.

We went to our back door and Mother saw us. She smiled and hugged us and said, "Did you have a good adventure?" We said we sure did. She brought out some cookies and milk without asking if we wanted them. She asked how we got along with the pancakes. We said just fine, but did not tell her about the potatoes. She asked if we slept at all and we laughed and said, "A little."

Baldy got his bike out of the barn and waved as he rode off. "So long," we said.

SHOWS

It is just about time to go back to school. In some ways I will be glad to see everybody and learn new things, but summer has been good. We did lots ourselves and we went to different kinds of shows, too. People bring entertaining acts to town for a while and then they go on to some other town. Our Opera House is big, with high ceilings and lots of folding seats. It has a stage with a pretty painted curtain in front and wings on the sides where people stand before they go on stage. It has dressing rooms on each side, one for men and one for women. Each room has an iron stove in it and there are two more stoves in the back of the big room. The ceiling is tin with raised patterns. The floor is hard wood.

Sometimes Lena High School or Warren High School puts on a play there and real actors come to town and give plays. They are always fun and interesting. Sometimes we are not sure what the play is about but we like to see the people acting and look at their make-up and watch to see if they make mistakes and have to be prompted. Somebody usually plays the piano. The high schools have orchestras.

They play while the scenery is being changed and between the acts.

Other times they show movies at the Opera House. It is near the Opera House Cafe in the middle of the main downtown block. The projection room for the moving picture projector is right at the top in the back of the opera house beside the balcony. The pictures I like best are about the Old West and cowboys and rustlers and Indians and cavalry soldiers. Bill Hart is a great cowboy. A lady plays the piano and when there is plenty of action she plays fast and loud. When it is quiet in the picture, or sad, or the man is making love to the lady, she plays soft and slow. We learn about cowboys and the Old West from the movies.

I think they also use the Opera House for big parties and for basketball games, but I have not seen any of those.

About the only other things they have downtown are the medicine shows, the bowery dances and the band concerts. In the summer they have band concerts at the bandstand every week. It is hot and people go to listen. They stand around or sit in cars or bring folding chairs. We kids sort of run around and listen, too. By Stadel's Dry Goods Store there is a drinking fountain on the side street, Center Street, across from the Lena Bank. Everybody uses the fountain when they are thirsty. Right next to it the popcorn wagon is parked. It is very fancy and pretty with brass and lights and new paint. Whenever there is anything going on downtown you can go to the window of the popcorn wagon and buy a sack of buttered popcorn for a nickel. He makes it all the time, so it is fresh.

Right in the popcorn wagon's place is where the medicine man parks his wagon when he comes to town. He does not come very often. His wagon is really a small truck that is painted very nice and has doors that open in back and a platform the man stands on to talk. A few days before they come to town for the show, he comes to get several of us boys to pass out handbills. He gives us each a big batch of these handbills telling when he will be in town to give a show and "let them buy" medicine. We spread the word around. He gives us 50 cents and we each take a different part of town and put the bills on people's porches and give them to people. It does not take very long.

When he is giving his show he has a pretty lady to help. Maybe she is his wife. He plays a one-man band with several instruments hung around his neck and drums on his waist and a mouth organ and a trumpet. He is really good and he makes a lot of noise so people are reminded to come see him. The lady sings and when he does a magic trick she helps him. As soon as there are enough people, he gets up on the platform at the back of the truck and tells them how wonderful his tonic is and how they will live long, healthy lives if they take it regularly. Then the lady picks up a basketful of bottles and sells them for a dollar each or six for five dollars. Everybody seems real serious about it. He tells how he got the formula from an old Indian chief who was a great medicine man. He says he spends most of his time gathering the special medicinal plants and roots and things that go in it. Dad says it is alot of "hokum" and that the tonic has alcohol in it.

The bowery dance is an open air dance on an outdoor floor across the street from Mr. Doll's Northside Garage, which is just back of Dr. Salter's house. They have it every Saturday night with a small band. Many young grown-up people come and dance. We kids don't spend much time there. It is usually too late at night. The music is peppy and sometimes we go listen for a while when they start.

We had Chatauqua in the tabernacle of the Camp Ground this summer. Mother says that is very high quality entertainment because the actors and speakers and singers are all well-trained and do their performances well enough so they can play in a big city. She took me to hear some singers, a Venetian Sextette and some light opera. She especially likes good music and it really was nice to hear. I could not believe how loud they could sing in that big tabernacle and still sound good. They were not really yelling, they were singing, and everybody could hear them all over. Mother told me one man was a very good singer and had a trained voice because it had a strong vibrato. It sounded wavery to me, but it was nice. She went to other programs, speakers and plays, but she did not think I would like them enough to sit on those hard benches that long. She was probably right.

Camp meeting has just finished. I don't suppose that is entertainment like a show, but it is different. People come from all over and camp in tents or stay in the dormitory for about ten days. Most of them are Methodists like we are. I have gone to Camp meeting in Fairmount, Indiana, where my Grandfather Hawkins is a minister. He and Gramma have a cottage.

Here in Lena we do not camp because we live so near the Camp Ground, but we go to the services. It is mostly serious church things, but the children and young people have fun, too. They have picnics and play games as well as study about the Bible and Jesus.

For us kids, the most fun of all summer was the tent show that set up in the pasture right north of our house. The cows were out and they cleaned things up enough so people could walk around without much trouble. It was set up by the Sherman Stock Company run by Mr. Robert Sherman. He was a friendly man and did not try to chase us off when we came to watch them raise the big tent. It was just like a circus tent and they had a little booth for a ticket office in front. Inside they had long benches and some folding chairs. They had their own platform for a stage and a curtain strung across in front. On each side were posters of Lena stores. I suppose it was advertising that the storekeepers paid for.

They charged children ten cents and adults forty cents to see a show. Before the show and between the acts they had a man and lady walking around selling candy and crackerjack. The plays were interesting, sometimes funny and sometimes very dramatic or scary. I don't remember all about them, but I always liked the comedian who talked before the shows and sometimes in between acts. Sometimes he would tell jokes with an accent, like Swedish or Jewish or German or Irish or Italian. The next day some of us would imitate the different accents.

Anyway, the shows were fun and the show people were nice, but the best was afterward. The day after they left, Woody and Baldy and I looked very carefully around where the ticket office had been and found nickels, dimes and quarters that had been lost in the grass.

Tomorrow I will go to the drugstore and the Midget and get theme books, school books, pencils, pens, and blotters and get ready to start the sixth grade. Miss Helen King will be my teacher and I already know her. She and her sister Alice live up the hill from us. She is friendly and kind and she knows a lot.

SADNESS

I have not written for a long time. There is something
real bad on my mind and I have not been able to
say anything about it. You see, Pal was my dog and
he was my friend, too. I loved him and he loved me
and always wanted to be with me hiking in the country
or playing with my friends or just sitting around. He
was a Beagle and liked to hunt. He was brave and
willing to fight for me if he thought anybody was
bothering me. He did not always understand, but if
he thought I was in trouble he didn't wait, he just
went right after whoever he thought might be trying
to hurt me. One time he came around a corner of
the house and saw me wrestling with a friend. He
was not hurting me but Pal thought he was. He ran
across the yard growling with his back hair standing
up. He jumped way up and hit my friend in the chest
and would have bitten him if I had not pulled Pal
off and quieted him down. He was lively and quick
and lots of times I could tell he was having fun because
he smiled while he had his tongue out and panted
with excitement.

A while ago Pal got sick. It was cold and wintery and he caught a disease. My dad is a doctor for people, but he took Pal to a veterinarian, who is a doctor for animals. They said Pal had distemper and they would do what they could but he was awful sick. He felt so bad. He just laid still and his nose was so dry and hot and he shivered and sometimes jerked a little. He did not want anything to eat. He tried to drink some water and they tried to give him some medicine, but it did not do any good. Pal died. Dad buried him in the backyard.

I couldn't help crying. I cried so hard I didn't think I could stop. Mother tried to make me feel better. She held me like she used to when I was little. She said animals never live very long and we have to realize that. But Pal was only three years old.

It is wonderful to be alive and know things, even hard and bad things. But there are so many good and nice and happy things that they can fill up most of the time. I don't see why people can't feel good and go on and on. But Mother said God has plans for every one of us and we cannot know what the plan is. We are supposed to do the best we know how as long as our bodies last and then our souls go to Heaven for ever and ever. I can't think how I could be in Heaven without my body. If they put my body in the ground, why doesn't that mean they put me in the ground, too? How could I get out to go to Heaven, even if I knew where it was?

I never thought about things like this before last summer. Another bad thing happened then. I did not write about it because I couldn't. That was when Grandfather Vickery died.

Grandfather's name was Francis Horn Vickery. Everybody called him Frank. He and Grandmother lived on a farm near Sheridan, Indiana. When I was little, but I can still remember it, Mother and Dad and I rode in a buggy from Fairmount, where I was born, to Grandfather's farm. It was a long trip and took all day. Dad held the reins and drove the horse and I sat up beside him. When I got tired Mother would hold me and let me sleep.

When we reached Grandfather's farm, he helped me down from the buggy and smiled and said, "I'm glad you got here all right. Let me look at you. My, you are growing so fast!" Grandmother came out, too, and she thought I was a nice boy and had been growing. It was fun on the farm. I had to watch out for some of the big animals, but Dad or Grandfather or Uncle Clem were always around to help me be careful. Uncle Clem had a farm across the road.

Grandfather was such a nice man. He was about the same size as my dad, which is medium for people, I guess. He had light yellowish hair and a reddish mustache with a little white in it. He was slim and strong and when he picked me up I could see his eyes better. They were blue and he had crinkly wrinkles beside them when he smiled. He was quiet and kind and he did not talk a lot but when he did it was pleasant and easy. My dad talked more than either Grandfather or Uncle Clem and it was fun to listen to him.

My mother and Aunt Hannah did most of the cooking and fixing meals because Grandmother was not very well. But the most fun for me was when they made ice cream. That was the men's job.

Grandfather had a favorite recipe. He put the milk and cream and sugar and vanilla and whatever else went in it together and put the mixture in the metal container with the paddles and set it all in the freezer. Uncle Clem had got chunks of ice from Great Uncle Joe Vickery, Grandfather's brother in Sheridan. It was in a gunny sack and Dad whacked it with the back of an ax to break it up so they could pack it in the freezer. Then they put rock salt on the ice and started to turn the crank. They all took turns and told me I could, too. I tried but I really did not move the handle very much. After a while they opened up the inside can to try the ice cream. That is the part I remember the best. It was so good I can still taste it.

I don't know how long we were there. We visited Grandfather and Grandmother other times, but not very many. I loved them both so much and I thought I could always go to visit them.

Then last summer there was a telephone call. My dad always answers the telephone because it is usually a patient that wants him to do something. This time Dad talked a long time and was very serious. When he was through, he said to Mother, "Father has died. It just happened a little while ago. He evidently went out to get the mail and had a heart attack on the way back. He died sitting under that big tree near the mail box."

He sat down with me and said, "Jack, you know how they tell you in Sunday school that people die and go to Heaven." I just looked at him. I was scared and did not know what to say. He said, "Well, that just now happened to Grandfather. There will be a funeral and we will go back home for it."

I knew that it was bad to be dead and that it was supposed to be nice to be in Heaven, but I did not know what a funeral was. I wanted to say something and I wanted to cry. I was all mixed up and did not know what to do. I wanted to ask if I would not ever see Grandfather anymore or if he would not talk to me anymore or if he wouldn't know me if he saw me or if I saw him. But I couldn't say anything. Mother patted me and said it would be all right and God would take care of everything, but I didn't see how it could be all right if I would not be able to visit Grandfather on his farm again. I couldn't say what I was thinking and Mother thought I just did not understand. And I guess I didn't.

We went back on the Illinois Central to Chicago and then the Monon to Indiana. Uncle Clem met us and took us back to Grandfather's house. In the living room up on stands was a big long box they called a coffin. Grandfather was in it lying down, partly covered up. His head was on a pillow and he looked almost like the last time I saw him but he was so still. I knew then that it was like when a bird or a rabbit is dead. They look about the same but they are all different and they never do anything again.

There were too many things to remember. Lots of people came. They had flowers. A minister told how good Grandfather was and how we would all see him again in Heaven. I don't know how he could know but I hope he does. Afterward Dad told me, "That was Grandfather's body, but he is not there. His spirit has gone on to Heaven and we believe that we will meet him there some day and that even if we don't have our same bodies, we will know each other and enjoy being together." I still did not understand how he could know that. He said, "Son, there are things we cannot know, but we believe and hope. This is one of our beliefs."

When we got back home, I thought about it a lot. Sometimes when I was supposed to be out playing I was just sitting somewhere with Pal and thinking about Grandfather and about what would happen to all the rest of us.

I could hug Pal and he would grin and pant and we would run and chase a bird or a butterfly or a rabbit and it would seem like things were all right again. Mother said we have to go ahead and be the best people we can and let God take care of things we cannot understand.

Now Pal is gone, too. I suppose sometime it will be almost all right again. I hope so. But right now I feel so bad about losing my grandfather and my friend Pal. And there is not really anything I can say to tell you how I feel.

TOOTHY'S VISIT

I don't think I wrote about my groundhog. We called him Toothy because he had big white front teeth and he showed them alot.

My dad was making a call out in the country one day, driving his Model T roadster. He has real narrow tires on the car. He calls them "three-inch tires." That way, he can drive the car anywhere a buggy can go, following the buggy tracks. Anyway, this wasn't too bad a day and the roads, which are mostly dirt or mud, were pretty good. Dad was going along at a good clip, maybe twenty miles an hour, when a woodchuck ran across the road in front of him. Groundhogs, or woodchucks, do not run very fast. Dad saw that he had gone into a hole in the ground but it was not deep enough. The woodchuck's tail hung out. So Dad stopped the car, ran to the woodchuck and grabbed him by the tail. He pulled him out of the hole, but the woodchuck was angry and he twisted and turned and tried to bite with his big teeth. Dad put him in the trunk of his car. He went on to make his call; then he came home and told me he had a woodchuck in the car. I ran out to see, and Dad got two pair of heavy gloves.

We put on the gloves. Dad opened the trunk and there was the woodchuck in a corner looking out at us. Dad was very quick. He grabbed the woodchuck by the head and neck and lifted him out. I got hold of the tail and pulled him so he could not scratch with his claws. Woodchucks have strong legs and feet for digging. We hauled him into the house and put him in the basement. Mother said, "What in the world is that?" Dad said, "I caught a groundhog. We'll get him out of the basement soon." Dad put a wooden box over him. Then he said, "Well, Jack, what will we do now? I thought maybe we could tame him for a pet."

I said, "Sure. Let's put a collar on him."

Dad said, "Yes, let's use one of Pal's old collars." I knew where it was, so I ran to get it. Then we put our gloves back on and Dad said, "I'll hold his head; you put the collar on." So I lifted up the box. Dad got both hands on the woodchuck's head, but not until he had some teeth marks in his gloves. He held the old fellow real tight and I put on the collar from the back, trying to keep out of the way of his feet and claws.

I buckled the collar on his neck. Then Dad said, "Let's put him in the old dog pen. We still had a fenced-in place with a little dog house. We tied a rope on his collar and put him in the pen and put some water in for him. After we went out he just sat there and looked at us and showed his big front teeth. Dad said, "He sure is a toothy one."

I said, "Hey, that's it. Let's call him Toothy."

Dad laughed and said, "That's fine. Toothy it is."

We tried very hard to be friendly with Toothy. We gave him water and different kinds of weeds and plants to eat. We talked nice to him and let him use Pal's old dog house. But he didn't understand. He just wanted to get away and be wild again. One night he chewed through his rope and dug under the fence and ran away. We never saw him again. I felt bad because I thought maybe he would be a pet, but I was kind of glad he got loose if that was what he really wanted.

Dad said, "You know, if anybody ever sees him, they will be surprised to see a woodchuck with a dog collar."

LONE SCOUTS

Here it is Christman vacation already. I have not
written anything except school work for several weeks.
It has been a busy fall. Sixth grade takes up a lot
of time and is really interesting, too. Miss Helen King
is our teacher. She is plump and friendly and nice,
but strict about school. The things I like best are
English, History, Physiology and Geography.
Arithmetic is all right. We write themes and those
are sort of fun because I have practiced them on my
own. Physiology and health and the human body
ought to be interesting to anybody, but I like them
because Dad is a doctor and maybe someday I might
be one, too. History can be dull if you only try to
learn the dates, but if you think of real people living
in olden times and how they lived and worked and
fought and made governments and what they thought
about, then it is interesting. Geography tells us about
our country and the world, what places are like and
what people do in them. I would like to travel and
visit all over the world some day. Arithmetic is
something we have to know and it is not too hard,

but I just don't like it as well as the other subjects. We have music, too, and that is always fun and easy.

Our music teacher is Miss Helene Dunn. She is young and tall, slender, brunette and pretty. She teaches music to the whole school. When it is time for music, we go upstairs to the music room. She has a piano there. She uses it to teach about the scales and chords and sometimes she plays while we sing songs. One of my favorites is "Tenting Tonight." It is about the Civil War soldiers camping during the war and it is sad. I would like to sing bass, but I can't get to the lowest notes. She plays symphony and operetta music on the Victrola phonograph and helps us pick out the different instruments and melodies so we can appreciate music better.

Thanksgiving and my birthday were last month. That was a good thing to remember. Mother fixed up a real turkey feast and had some of my friends over for dinner. I ate so much I suppose I should be embarrassed, but it was so good I just remember it as a wonderful celebration.

What I am most excited about is Lone Scouts. On my birthday, November 27, I was eleven years old. That is old enough to join Lone Scouts of America and I had been looking forward to that for a long time. My friends and I have been reading about Boy Scouts for a year or two. Roy Blakeley, Pee Wee Harris and all their friends, and even Tom Swift, are real to us because we have read so many of the books about them. Dad gets me some and I buy some for fifty cents each and some of them I borrow from the library. Whenever I go to the Lena Library upstairs in the town hall, Miss Kathryn Krape, the librarian, tells me right away if there is a new Boy Scout book or a new copy of Boy's Life magazine.

The only thing is, a boy has to be twelve years old to be a Boy Scout, but only eleven to be a Lone Scout. Anyway, there is no Boy Scout troop in Lena. If we want to be Scouts, Lone Scouts are the only kind we can be. Woody, Baldy, Aaron, Barton, Waldo, Willard and Dale are friends who are most eager to be Scouts. I am the first one who has actually joined, but the others are looking at my manuals and books and I know they will join soon. Then we can form a Tribe. It takes five boys to make a Tribe and they have to have a grown-up man to sponsor them and teach them.

My dad says that Scouting is great and he will help us. Scouting started in England in 1908 when Lt. General Sir Robert S.S. Baden Powell wrote SCOUTING FOR BOYS and organized it. I read that he had been a war hero in the Boer War in South Africa and saved the city of Mafeking. One of the reasons he was so resourceful was that he had always liked the outdoors and studied how to be self-reliant. After the war he came home and thought boys would like to know some of the things he had learned, especially how to enjoy the outdoors. He told about doing good turns for people and also many other things about being healthy and strong and good citizens.

Very soon after, Scouting came to America. W.C. Boyce, a businessman from Chicago, was in London and became lost in a bad fog. A boy offered to help him, took him to where he wanted to go, then would not take money for it. He said, "I am a Boy Scout, and we do not take pay for doing good turns." Mr. Boyce thought that was a great idea and asked the boy to tell him more about it. The boy told him more and also put him in touch with the Boy Scout Headquarters. Mr. Boyce came home and helped organize the Boy Scouts of America. Nobody knows the name of the Scout who helped him. Mr. Boyce is the Chief Totem of the Lone Scouts of America and their address is 500 North Dearborn Street, Chicago, Illinois.

Ernest Thompson Seton and Daniel Carter (Uncle Dan) Beard had formed organizations something like the Scouts here in the United States. When the Boy Scouts were organized, they joined to make the whole thing stronger. They are both very skillful in Indian craft and lore and they wrote and illustrated books that boys like.

I have been spending a lot of time reading and studying the Lone Scout Degree books. They tell about nature and the outdoors and how to make camp and use camping tools. They also tell about so many other things that a boy could almost plan his life by these books. It is different from school, and different from Sunday school, but it is important, too.

My dad helps me with the Lone Scout program. If there is something I don't understand or something I need to do, he helps me. He said that he started a Scout troop, back when Scouts were brand new, in a town in Indiana where he was a pastor, before he became a doctor. So he has known about Scouting almost from the beginning. He says that when more of my friends have joined and are ready, we will start a Tribe and will meet in my shack. I think that is a great idea and so do they. We are all working on it.

The Lone Scout program has seven degrees. The first three are in the Teepee Lodge, the next three are in the Totem Pole Lodge and the seventh degree is in the Sagamore Lodge. Sagamore is the highest, of course, and it is concerned with woodcraft, pioneering and camping. I am just on the first degree and that means I have to study and work on exercising, deep breathing, rules for good health, knowledge of the body and how it works, general knowledge of the five senses and how the body is controlled and used. I have to know how the body is nourished, develop powers of observation and description (including making drawings), improve sight and hearing, learn the National Anthem, learn the principles of courtesy that mark the gentleman, and perform daily chores and duties cheerfully. I must memorize, "The Word of Honor of a Lone Scout Is as True as Steel and as Good as Gold," strive to see the good in others and to have charity for all men, seek out five opportunities to do an act of special kindness toward an animal, and resolve never to be cruel to helpless beasts. I will make a top or kite or something similar, putting into it the best of my ability, learn how to make a good map and take a hike of a mile and make notes that will enable me to draw a proper road map on my return home. Those are the twenty tests of the first degree. You can see why I have been busy trying to learn all that outside of school.

The second degree will get started on woodcraft and astronomy, the third patriotism and more woodcraft, the fourth bird study, signalling and first aid, and so on to more advanced wood lore, life saving, animal studies and citizenship. Every Scout studies and does the things he is supposed to and when he has finished a degree, sends a report to headquarters. Then he gets a pin with a design that shows the degree he has earned. We can buy uniforms just like the Boy Scouts. There is a khaki campaign hat, shirt, tie, neckerchief, breeches, puttees and shoes. There are special places to wear the badges and the patches that tell what tribe a Scout belongs to.

We are trying hard to learn as much as we can, but we have fun, too. We get together already to study or do things and then we usually end up playing a game or going for some sort of hike. Different boys come over at different times.

About two weeks ago Baldy came and we were studying the part about walking quietly in the woods, putting one foot directly in front of the other, toeing in and stepping on the front part of the foot first. We went out in the woods in the back of our lot to practice. He was pretty good at sneaking up on me, but whenever I tried to sneak up on him, even if I did not break any twigs or scrape anything, my right ankle always made a cracking sound and he could tell I was coming.

Then we went in my shack and studied about courtesy and being a gentleman. This comes down from King Arthur's knights who were very tough and rugged, but kind and gentle to ladies and children. We read about this, then decided to go out and practice being knights. We each cut a branch about three feet long and made a sword out of it. Then we fenced and dueled for a while. We got poked a little but nothing that hurt very much.

We wanted to be knights on horseback in a jousting tournament, but we could not think of anything to use for shields. We did not want to take the time to make them. Then I thought, how about the outdoor toilet seat lids. They were only about a foot and a half square, but they were loose and they had hand holds on top. So we each got one and then ran at each other as if we were on horseback, using our swords as lances. We really tried to hit the shields instead of sticking each other, but the lances skidded off some. After several runs we had bruises, but neither of us was bleeding. We decided we were about even and we might as well go save a damsel from a dragon. We could not find either one, so we went back to the shack to read a little more and then it was time for supper.

Maybe by next summer we can really get organized into a Tribe. Dad thinks we can. Anyway, we are learning more about Lone Scouting. If we can hold together, maybe we could even start a Boy Scout Troop sometime. They had a troop in Lena about eight years ago, but it only lasted a year or two. Mr. W.C. Lutz, the jeweler and school janitor, was the Scoutmaster. Dad thinks Mr. Lutz might try it again if enough people want him to.

Christmas is coming soon. I should not be selfish, thinking about presents, but I hope this year Mother and Dad give me parts of the Scout uniform.

HOUSE CALL

Dad and I just got back from a call to see a patient at home. He is a man who is terribly sick and he lives near Waddams Grove. It is winter, but the road is shoveled and plowed out. It is a sunny Sunday afternoon and Dad asked if I would ride along with him. I said yes right away because I like to ride with him whenever I can. We don't get much other chance to talk.

We rode in the Dodge sedan. It is a strong car and can go over High Point without shifting gears when the road is dry. Today there were slippery spots and soft places, so Dad had to shift into low a few times. It has a heater that keeps it warm inside.

On the way, Dad said, "This patient has lobar pneumonia. That means a whole lobe or section of a lung is infected. He has it on both sides, so it is double lobar pneumonia. He has a high fever, coughs and feels weak and miserable."

"Will he get well?" I asked.

"I don't know for sure," Dad said, "but he is a strong man with no bad habits and I think he is holding his own now. I have been seeing him every

241

day. His wife and daughter are good at nursing him and his son is taking care of the farm work. It is lucky he doesn't have to worry about that."

"What difference would the farm work make?" I asked. "He can't do it anyway."

"That's right, but it helps a person fight illness if he doesn't have to worry about other things. If people are upset and concerned about troubles it seems like they don't have as much strength to get well with. Diseases are different. In this kind of pneumonia, if the patient is going to get well, he is likely to go through a crisis. He gets awfully sick and feverish and then rapidly gets a lot better. If they do that, they nearly always go ahead and get well."

"What can a doctor do to help?" I asked.

He said, "Well, first we examine the patient to find out as best we can what is the matter. In a case of pneumonia we use aspirin and sometimes quinine for the fever, iodized calcium to help loosen the cough and cough medicines with some codeine or morphine if we need to stop excessive coughing. Sometimes we use honey or hard candy to soothe the throat. We warm the chest with mustard plasters and flannel and use hot water bottles whenever he feels chilly. His wife keeps him clean and as comfortable in bed as she can. Soups are about all he can eat, but they are good for him. There are other things. Nearly half of these patients do not get well no matter how hard we all work and pray."

We rode awhile and he got through some mushy places in the road. Then I asked him, "Dad, don't you feel bad when a patient dies? How can you stand that?"

He said, "Yes, Jack, I feel bad—I want to help every patient to get well and I try as hard as I can to help them all. But I know and they know that everybody dies sometime. If we all do our best, then we have to accept the outcome as God's will. That helps me. You must understand that no matter how a doctor feels, he must always keep a clear head. He cannot help the patient unless his brain is working right."

We were nearly at the farm house. I had one question I really wanted to ask. "Dad," I said, "I know it is hard to be a doctor, and lots of work. Do you really like being a doctor?"

We were turning into the barnyard and he was looking for a place to stop so we could get out again. "Yes," he said, "I like being a doctor. All my life I wanted to help people and I think this is the best way to do it. There are things I would change if I could. I get too tired sometimes. But, yes, being a physician is what I always wanted."

I waited in the car for a while, then I went to the barn and looked around from the outside. There was a big dog and a couple of cats and they all wanted to rub against me to get warm. I opened the door just a little to see the cows in their stalls and a couple of horses in box stalls. It was warm in the barn from the heat of the animals, but I did not go in. After a while I went back to sit in the car.

I thought about Dad in the house examining the patient and listening to the family telling what all had happened since yesterday. Then he would tell them what medicine to use and how to look after the patient till he comes again tomorrow. Dad really likes people.

He is cheerful and jokes with them and remembers all about them.

Lots of times it is hard for Mother because he is gone so much. She has to take care of the house and my sisters and me and everything. But when Dad comes home, even if he is tired and she is, too, things seem brighter and soon he makes everybody happy. I am glad he can help sick people and it makes me feel sort of warm and proud down inside that patients want him to help them and he is willing to do it. Maybe I can't see him as much as other kids see their dads, but when I do, like today, it is really special.

I was wondering what I would have to do to be a doctor like my dad. I know I have to do good work in school and keep going to school a long time. When we lived in Valparaiso, Dad was in medical school and he taught me many names of human anatomy and something about physiology and pathology. His friends thought that was great, but I don't remember it very well now. They all laughed one time when they asked me where my dad was and I said that he was studying his "ologies."

Soon Dad came out carrying his big black bag. He was smiling as he jumped in the car and started the engine. "Jack," he said, "I believe he has passed the crisis. His fever broke this morning, he looks stronger, and he is getting some appetite. I believe he will get well." I could see that he was really happy and that he didn't care how much work it was if the patient would just get well.

About all I said on the way home was, "Dad, I want to be a doctor. Just like you."

HOUSE CALL

He squeezed my hand. "You can, Jack," he said,
"If you really want to. I would be proud."

PHOTOGRAPHS

Rev. Grandfather Hawkins

Gramma and Me

All dressed up Age 4

Lee Otis Vickery, M. D.
(My Dad)

Winter Fun

Dad and Mom and the new Dodge

Eugene Livingstone Vickery
(Dad calls me Jack)

Marthene and Eugene - Twin Cousins

My Sisters Virginia and Margerr

Dad and Me

Uncle Dan Reed

Me with Grandmother Rhoda Ann V.

- The End -